MOTIVATIONAL DESIGN

The Secret to Producing Effective Children's Media

Marilyn P. Arnone

THE SCARECROW PRESS, INC.
Lanham, Maryland • Toronto • Oxford
2005

SCARECROW PRESS, INC.

Published in the United States of America
by Scarecrow Press, Inc.
A wholly owned subsidiary of
The Rowman & Littlefield Publishing Group, Inc.
4501 Forbes Boulevard, Suite 200, Lanham, Maryland 20706
www.scarecrowpress.com

PO Box 317
Oxford
OX2 9RU, UK

Copyright © 2005 by Marilyn P. Arnone

All rights reserved. No part of this publication may be reproduced, stored in a retrieval system, or transmitted in any form or by any means, electronic, mechanical, photocopying, recording, or otherwise, without the prior permission of the publisher.

British Library Cataloguing in Publication Information Available

Library of Congress Cataloging-in-Publication Data

Arnone, Marilyn P.
  Motivational design : the secret to producing effective children's media / Marilyn P. Arnone.
    p. cm.
  Includes bibliographical references and index.
  ISBN 0-8108-5037-0 (alk. paper)
  1. Children's mass media. 2. Motivation (Psychology) in children. I. Title.
P94.5.C55.A76 2005
302.23'083—dc22

2004011085

Printed in the United States of America

∞™ The paper used in this publication meets the minimum requirements of American National Standard for Information Sciences—Permanence of Paper for Printed Library Materials, ANSI/NISO Z39.48-1992.

To Gerry Lesser, Harvard University,
and John Keller, Florida State University

CONTENTS

Foreword vii

Introduction ix

PART 1   MOTIVATION AND CHILDREN'S MEDIA

1 Motivation: What Is It, Exactly? 3

2 The CTW Model 9

3 The ARCS Model 23

4 An Integrative and Systematic Approach 37

PART 2   MOTIVATIONAL STRATEGIES FOR CHILDREN'S MEDIA

5 Gaining and Sustaining Attention 49

6 Establishing Relevance 63

7 Building and Reinforcing Confidence 75

8 Promoting Satisfaction (and a Continuing Motivation to Learn) 95

9 Guidelines, Mandates, and Considerations for Convergence Media 107

PART 3 USING THE CTW AND ARCS MODELS TO REDESIGN A CHILDREN'S TV PROGRAM (A CASE STUDY)

10	A Local Phenomenon	121
11	Rescue Efforts	125
12	The Role of Formative Evaluation	143
13	A Few Closing Thoughts	155

Appendix A: WebMAC for Children's TV Websites — 157

Appendix B: WebMAC for Children's TV Websites: Administrator Directions, Scoring Guidelines, Score Sheets, and Grids — 163

Index — 171

About the Author — 177

FOREWORD

When Marilyn Arnone first shared a draft of her manuscript with me, I had an immediate positive reaction. At first glance the book had visual appeal, the formatting techniques for highlighting key conventions such as tips and tactics were eye-catching, and I could see that the book had a good blend of practical and applied components. Now I am delighted to have been asked to write a foreword for this book.

If you know or ever meet Marilyn, you'll certainly see her personality reflected in this book. Her rich performance background, her creative talents and optimism, her understanding of the scholarly material reflected in this book, and her ability to communicate contribute to making sure this book accomplishes the difficult challenge of fusing practice and theory. It's truly useful for people who design learning materials and environments, whether in multimedia or more conventional settings, yet also serves as a primer for people who don't have formal knowledge of human motivation. Marilyn introduces the essential attributes of many motivational concepts in a manner that makes their meaning easy to grasp without being distorted or diluted. Furthermore, she includes countless examples from her personal experience and other settings to provide readers with concrete anchors and stimulate their own thoughts about how to identify and achieve motivational goals in design.

In addition to my pleasure in reading such a well-written, interesting, and useful book, I'm pleased by the contribution it makes to the literature of motivational design. The distinction between motivational research and motivational design is not well established in the literature. Generally, a separation is made between scholars and practitioners; scholars introduce practical strategies based on inferences from the results of their research, and practitioners either try to apply these strategies or write books about a collection of successful practices. In my development and use of the ARCS model of motivational design, I almost never use the word *practitioners* because it implies that one is simply applying established principles and techniques. In contrast, I prefer the term *problem solvers* because one is seldom able to just apply motivational principles; the principles have to be adapted and implemented innovatively, depending on unique aspects that are always part of real life (as opposed to laboratory situations). Marilyn's book certainly falls into the realm of supporting a problem-solving approach to motivational design.

The book begins, appropriately for its intended audience, with material about motivation and the things that are important for children's media producers. The content of the book is grounded in the design approaches suggested by the Children's Television Workshop (CTW) model and are reflected in the examples she includes. Then she guides readers through the various parts of the ARCS model, with many examples to anchor each element in concrete experience. She provides enough theoretical information on key motivational concepts and theories, children's developmental stages, and research summaries to enable readers to understand the "why" of each aspect of motivational design, not just the "how." And she includes many practical guidelines and suggestions, some in the form of "tips and tactics." All of this is incorporated into the final part of the book, a case study that provides a "practice what you preach" example.

I expect that a great many people will find their way to this book, not just children's media producers. Why? Because the approach, contents, appeal, and utility cut across various areas of application. Congratulations to Marilyn on an excellent contribution to knowledge.

—John M. Keller, Ph.D., professor of
educational psychology and learning systems,
Florida State University

INTRODUCTION

There are no new ideas. There are only new combinations of existing ideas—sparks that ignite when a relationship between ideas comes together in an enlightening way. That's the philosophy expressed in James Webb Young's succinct little book *A Technique for Producing Ideas* (1940). A lot of people agree with him; I know I do. This book is a case in point. It exists because of the ideas of two people who have influenced me in my work: Gerry Lesser from Harvard University and John Keller from Florida State University (FSU).

Dr. Gerry Lesser was my adviser a number of years ago (don't make me say how many) when I was a student at Harvard University's Graduate School of Education. My focus at that time was research in children's television and human development. Lesser was one of the chief architects of the immensely successful *Sesame Street* and adviser to the Children's Television Workshop (CTW). He has since played a role in the success of numerous other children's programs, both national and international. I learned the CTW model for designing children's television programs from him. That model can be applied to the design of most children's media projects.

Dr. John Keller, a professor at FSU, is the creator of the ARCS model of motivational design. His model draws on the work of numerous others, as it is solidly grounded in motivation theory, yet he came up with a systematic way of using theory to prescribe practical motivational strategies that educators can use to enhance instruction.

A few years ago, I was working on a project for children that had numerous media components—television, Web, and print. I was planning, as usual, to use the CTW model as I generally did in children's media development. An important objective of the program was to encourage children's creative efforts in art as well as build confidence. Because these objectives had such a strong motivational emphasis, I decided to use the ARCS model as a "motivation overlay" to the CTW model. I couldn't have been more pleased with the results, and I've been doing it ever since. If you don't address motivation as a crucial component, whatever you are producing educationally for children might not succeed in achieving your learning objectives.

I think you will discover that a combination of these two tried-and-true models results in a systematic, efficient, and powerful approach for developing educational and entertaining children's media materials that will stimulate your young audience's motivation to learn.

WHO THIS BOOK IS FOR ...

Anyone who produces media content for children will benefit from reading this book, including television and multimedia producers, communications students learning the ropes of television, video and multimedia producers or Web developers, writers, and educators designing media materials for the classroom. For each of these audiences, motivating children to watch, interact, and learn from the media they develop is crucial. Some may have experience in developing educational objectives that can later be measured, but few have experience in assessing the motivational profile of their audience, developing motivational objectives, designing motivating strategies, and evaluating their effectiveness.

WHAT THIS BOOK IS AND IS NOT

This book is a practical guide, not a comprehensive compendium of research on children's media, motivation theory, or child development, though all are discussed generally as they apply to motivational strategies. Students of media studies and television, video, and film production will find it a handy companion to their regular texts as they begin to develop production ideas they will later produce. Video and interactive media producers will appreciate the book as a way to spark their own ideas during

INTRODUCTION   xi

project development. Educators will recognize that their roles frequently demand the skills of a media producer.

ASSUMPTIONS

The audience for this book is made up of busy people, so it is intentionally compact, although it will send you in the right direction if you are looking to delve deeper into any one area discussed.

The book assumes that the children's media productions you are planning have education as their overarching goal. Yet education will often not happen in the absence of entertainment value.

Finally, because its intended audience includes students and educators, this book assumes that not everyone has a big media budget. Many of us have to be very creative in finding ways to accomplish our goals on shoestring budgets. Throughout the text, you will find tips on accomplishing economically what could otherwise cost a lot of money.

CONVENTIONS USED IN THIS BOOK

This practical guide includes feature sections sprinkled throughout the chapters to provide you with quick specific information on a number of topics. These conventions are described in the following table:

Icon	What It Means
 **Tips and Tactics**	**Tips and Tactics** can be snippets of advice to make your job as a children's media producer easier, or tactics and strategies for incorporating motivation into your media project.
 **Take 2**	**Take 2!** encapsulates motivational principles and concepts and explains key terms or jargon.
	**Developmental Snapshots** provide descriptive snapshots of children at different ages.
 **Watch Out!**	**Watch Out!** alerts you to possible problems and pitfalls.

 **Theoretically Speaking** provides additional information on some of the motivation theories described.

 **The Research Says** provides empirical support for some of the content presented.

Acknowledgments

At the top of my list of acknowledgments are John Keller and Gerry Lesser, whose work provided the inspiration for this book. I would also like to thank my friend and colleague Ruth Small for reading the chapters and providing knowledgeable feedback. Thanks also to MariRae Dopke, especially for her suggestions regarding the case study in part 3. Thanks to my parents, Len and Gladys Mathieu, for their welcome comments and cheerful encouragement during the process. Finally, I am very grateful to my husband, Joe Arnone, for his valuable input on a number of chapters, but most importantly for his love and support along the way.

Part I

MOTIVATION AND CHILDREN'S MEDIA

1

MOTIVATION: WHAT IS IT, EXACTLY?

Motivated: it's what professors want their students to feel about the subject they are teaching. It's what networks want viewers to be when watching their programs and what advertising executives want potential customers to be when purchasing the products they promote through those outrageous ad campaigns. It's what we want our kids to feel as they study for their science midterm (or when we ask them to clean their room). As the parent of a teenage girl, I realize that the motivation to excel on either of those tasks may be severely lacking. My daughter is, however, very motivated to ride horses. She is even willing to clean stalls every weekend in exchange for additional riding lessons. That motivation comes from within.

What is this fuzzy thing we call motivation? Simply put, motivation explains why we choose to expend effort on some things and not others. While this explanation may sound simple, motivation is complex and involves many individual variables that affect the direction and intensity of behavior. We'll get to some of those.

Effort implies movement, whether mental or physical. There is movement, then, in motivation. For readers interested in word origins, motivation comes from the Latin word *movere,* which means to move. In the case of getting her room cleaned, my daughter "moves" because she has to! The horse thing, on the other hand, is intrinsically motivated. The more she learns about riding, the better she rides. And she loves to ride, and ride well.

As Media Producers, Our Job Is to Motivate!

There are variations in the definition of motivation, but the dictionary definition is pretty good. It means "to stimulate to action; provide with an incentive or motive; impel; incite." (American Heritage Dictionary)

THE TWO ESSENTIAL INGREDIENTS

Research shows that motivation consists of two factors: (1) valuing the task at hand and (2) expecting that you can be successful at it. If either factor is missing, you will likely not be motivated to tackle the task at hand. This is especially true when there is a choice involved. My daughter is not compelled to engage in equestrian studies. She does so because she finds personal fulfillment (value) in it and she knows she can be good at it (expectation for success). On the other hand, she does not see the value of cleaning her room even though she possesses the basic organizational skills for doing so.

Do the Math!

1 (Value) × 0 (No Expectation for Success) = 0 (Unmotivated)
0 (No Value) × 1 (Expectation for Success) = 0 (Unmotivated)
1 (Value) × 1 (Expectation for Success) = **Motivated**

INTRINSIC VERSUS EXTRINSIC MOTIVATION

Consider also that motivation can come from within (intrinsic) or without (extrinsic). Intrinsic motivation is powerful, as my daughter's example demonstrates. As a media producer, you can tap into a child's intrinsic motivation to learn. You will discover lots of strategies in chapters 4–8. For now, consider these possibilities:

- Know your audience well. For example, consider how the interests of the three-year-old differ from those of the eight-year-old.
- Provide choices. This may be easier for print and interactive media, but it's still possible for video, as we'll discover later.
- Allow active involvement.
- Capitalize on children's love of games.
- Stimulate a child's natural curiosity.

What is intrinsically or extrinsically motivating to a child is, in part, influenced by developmental factors. Look at the "snapshot" of the child at three, following. What motivates her? While this book is not about child development, it includes a developmental snapshot in each chapter in parts 1–2, as a trigger for thinking about motivational opportunities and challenges posed by the developing child.

**Developmental Snapshot
The Child at Three**

Children at three can accomplish their daily routines with apparent ease. They are gaining more control of themselves and enjoy the feeling of competency. They love interacting with people, and, in contrast with a two-year-old's possessive behavior, the three-year-old will happily share a prized possession to ensure acceptance. Language ability improves dramatically and the three-year-old enjoys playing with language, practicing words, talking, and listening to herself speak. ("The Child at Four" is in chapter 2.)

Note: Developmental snapshots are necessarily general and do not take into consideration wide variations in individual differences related to personality, learning, or physical development.

Extrinsic motivation can also be effective. Rewards are a common extrinsic incentive and they can include both physical and social rewards. For example, a children's website might include a downloadable software application of interest as a reward for completing a survey (physical). Another site might provide recognition for accomplishing a goal, such as displaying a child's artwork in an online art gallery with other children's art (social).

While extrinsic rewards are often useful, in some instances they can interfere with intrinsic motivation. More on this later.

Ideally, motivation comes from within, even though we may speak of "external" motivators. As a producer for children's media, you can use your skills and knowledge to seek out the motivation that lies within the child.

CREATING VALUE AND EXPECTATION FOR SUCCESS

How do you create value and an expectation for success in children? You can start by developing a safe and supportive environment in which you address the educational objectives of your production, whether it is electronic or print based.

Value

Appeal to individual differences. We'll find out how to do this later on.
Incorporate role models your audience can identify with.
Start with familiar concepts and work from there.

Expectation for Success

Show how effort will lead to success.
Present content in an easy to difficult sequence.
Break up your media content into small chunks.
Provide a means for guidance.

Use brainstorming whenever possible. (Yes, this can even be done with linear videos!)
Introduce cognitive conflict (or dissonance).
More to come . . .

Be clear about the purpose of your media product. Convey what is expected of your users/viewers as a result of watching and interacting with your media product.
More to come . . .

From there you can zero in on specific factors that help a child discover the value of what you are presenting and come to the realization that success is within reach. Without giving away too much of what you will discover in the chapters to follow, here are a few things to be thinking about.

HOW DO YOU MEASURE MOTIVATION?

We will examine a number of ways to measure the effectiveness of the media you develop in attaining its motivational objectives. The most direct measure of motivation is *effort*.

The concepts presented in this chapter are based on the work of Vroom and others in expectancy-value (E-V) theory, which has its roots in business and industry. It was later applied in teaching situations and has proven effective in designing and evaluating Web-based projects, as well. More about using E-V theory with Web-based projects in chapter 9.

FINAL POINT

There are many motivational theories, and this book provides a basic introduction to several of them. Interestingly, many motivational theories and principles can be framed within the intuitive perspective of E-V theory. You will see how in later chapters.

PRODUCER'S CHECKLIST FOR CHAPTER 1

- ❏ Motivation explains why a person chooses to put forth effort in a task.
- ❏ As producers, our job is to motivate—help children find their own motivation for learning or performing a task.
- ❏ Intrinsic motivation results from engaging in an activity for its own sake; extrinsic motivation is a result of external forces. Ultimately all lasting motivation comes from within.
- ❏ A child must both value the task or learning activity and expect to be successful at it in order to expend effort or persist in an activity. This principle applies no matter which medium you plan to deliver your message in.
- ❏ The best measure of motivation is *effort*.

DIGGING DEEPER

Those interested in delving into more depth on E-V theory can find a forty-page chapter on expectancy-value models of motivation in Pintrich and Schunk's book. Chapter 3 will include additional references.

Pintrich, Paul R., and Schunk, Dale H. 2002. *Motivation in Education: Theory, Research, and Applications*, 51–91. 2d ed. Upper Saddle River, N.J.: Merrill Prentice-Hall.

2

THE CTW MODEL

CTW stands for Children's Television Workshop, which recently changed its name to Sesame Workshop. The CTW model, which is used in the design, development, and evaluation of the many CTW programs, is the subject of this chapter. What distinguishes this model from others is its pioneering fusion of production, content, and research.

In the "old" (pre-CTW) days, there was a distinct difference between children's entertainment television and educational television. Many kids avoided watching "educational" television because it wasn't any fun. Then came CTW, and children's television hasn't been the same since. In the late 1960s, children became enraptured with Bert and Ernie, Big Bird, and a great cast of human characters that faithfully visited their homes five days a week to entertain and, yes, educate them. Over thirty years later, the CTW lineup of educational programs is still winning the hearts and loyalties of children in every age-group.

How did CTW arrive at the magical combination that entertained children and educated them at the same time? Initially it was the insight, creativity, and perseverance of Joan Ganz Cooney, Gerry Lesser, and Lloyd Morrisset who dreamed it could be done. Numerous others helped them realize their dream by building a strong foundation for the successful merger of education and entertainment. Cooney, a producer with an education background, and Morrisett, a psychologist and Carnegie Foundation executive, had a big vision and backed it with a solid action-based proposal that attracted an unprecedented $8 million in funding to support a two-year television project. Lesser, who had helped with the research components of the proposal, went to work to create the model.

ON MY WAY TO DISCOVERING THE CTW MODEL

I had always loved children's television and dreamed of working in it. As a young woman just finishing my undergraduate program at Emerson College in Boston, Massachusetts, I had the opportunity to work with the late, great Buffalo Bob Smith and Clarabel the Clown on the revival of Buffalo Bob's old NBC program, *The Howdy Doody Show* (see figure 1). The revival show was called *The NEW Howdy Doody Show* and was taped in Miami, Florida. Working on that program was great fun. When I wasn't on-camera as a character, I was on the puppet bridge with Pady Blackwood, the show's master puppeteer, working the marionettes. I also spent endless hours in the editing rooms watching the programs come together under the creative direction of Errol Falcon. The new show had bigger and better sets, a large audience in the Peanut Gallery, and an orchestra of top New York City musicians. We taped 130 shows that were syndicated nationally. There was something missing, though. For all its good intentions and positive messages, the program did not include a single education person on its staff. There was no one who really knew children. At that time my background was television and radio, not education, but I knew that was a flaw. I would have loved the series to last another year or so, but it was probably better for me that I moved on. I was about to discover the CTW model.

LESSONS FROM LESSER

When I came home to Boston after finishing the series, I investigated the program at the Harvard Graduate School of Education called (at that time) Research in Children's Television and Human Development. A partnership existed between CTW and the Harvard University Center for Research in Children's Television for the purpose of conducting research related to children's learning and visual media. The program was exactly what I was looking for, and I was accepted as a master's student with Gerry Lesser as my adviser. It was one of the best decisions I ever made. Through the years, I have used the CTW model with numerous children's media projects including television, video, and print.

THE CTW MODEL

Figure 1. Howdy Doody and me on the set of *The New Howdy Doody Show*

A Different Way of Approaching Children's Media Development

In 1967, for the first time in the history of television, producers, researchers, scholars, and educators were brought together under the direction of Gerry Lesser as pioneers in a brand-new television experiment. (No one really knew if it would work.) Lesser served as chairman of the board of advisers. They plugged away over five separate seminars designing the curriculum and program features of *Sesame Street*. Many outsiders scoffed at the idea that this mix of individuals could work together productively. After all, they came from such widely divergent disciplines that reaching agreement on program goals, to say nothing of curriculum and production issues, could hardly be expected. The naysayers were proven wrong when the outcome was a phenomenal success. Those seminars were the beginning of an era that lifted children's television to a new level.

In the foreword of Lesser's book *Children and Television: Lessons from Sesame Street,* Cooney credits Lesser's know-how, personality, and patience (along with the director of research, Ed Palmer) with winning over the production team. She credits the production team with daring to pursue an innovative approach. Incidentally, it would be worth your while to read the book for Lesser's rich accounts of each aspect of the model and lessons learned in the process of developing *Sesame Street*. It is out of print, but you can still obtain it from several online bookstores.

**Development Snapshot
The Child at Four**

Have you interacted with four-year-olds? If you have, you know that four-year-olds can be a challenge for parents and caregivers. They often seem irrepressible! Their behavior can be wild with almost constant physical activity of one kind or another. They now have more muscle coordination and greater physical abilities and they are not afraid to show them off! Bathroom humor is at a premium and downright insolence is not uncommon. Fortunately, the closer to four and a half and five the child moves, the less unmanageable he becomes and the more we start to see the question-asking behavior emerge—Why this? Why that? ("The Child at Five" is in chapter 3.)

Note: Developmental snapshots are necessarily general and do not take into consideration wide variations in individual differences related to personalities, learning, or physical development.

Educators who work with creative talent, including writers, producers, and artists, experience challenges. Lesser describes how feathers were ruffled as, for example, the educators seemed to overanalyze a creative idea. After all, the expertise of one member could be unfamiliar territory for another. Yet all had something valuable to offer to the mix, and on that they agreed. In time, the members of this blended group learned from one another and became an effective working unit. The most important lesson learned from this first venture was that educators and media types could work side by side toward a successful outcome. It has become the key premise of the CTW model. Readers who grew up on *Sesame Street* will understand how well this initial experiment turned out from both educational and entertainment perspectives because they experienced it.

By the time I arrived as a graduate student, the CTW model had proven its effectiveness, with CTW expanding its preschool program offerings to target the needs of school-age children. Its media portfolio had expanded beyond television and included print and other nonbroadcast materials.

Tips and Tactics

So, You Have a Very Small Budget

You may be saying by now, "I can't possibly do anything like CTW. They received mega bucks in grants for their first project. I have very little funding ... but a lot of heart!" Yes, you can. I know you can because I have. You can put together an advisory board for your project consisting of individuals with expertise in the areas that are pertinent to your children's media project. You might not be able to fly them in from around the country and put them up in hotels, but there are other options. (Meeting online has become a viable option we'll consider later.) Research the faculty at local or regional colleges and universities. Identify those who may be able to contribute their knowledge. Include parents too. If your budget cannot afford a small honorarium for participation, you can always ask for volunteers if you and your team have identified a real need and have some good ideas as a starting place.

APPLYING THE CTW MODEL TO YOUR PROJECT

Planning

Whether this is referred to as front-end analysis, needs assessment, preliminary research, or something else, the purpose of planning is to collect and analyze as much general background information as possible on the area you plan to address with your project. The need you have identified must be clarified and supported by research, especially as it applies to your target audience. That means staying current on a variety of children's issues through professional journals, trade publications, and conference proceedings available in print or online. You should be familiar with the media preferences of your audience (you may also consider conducting surveys and interviews with members of the target audience) and aware of possible competitive projects. This information-gathering phase could also include informal interviews with teachers, parents, and experts who could add insight to the problem you plan to address. Your project team should include individuals with strengths pertinent to your project. Together, you will develop a strong proposal with support from the literature, statistics, and leaders from the community or field. The need you plan to address must be convincing and your planning and preparation thorough, if you hope to attract funding for your project.

Selecting an Advisory Board

You are now ready to invite participants to your advisory board. How you attract your advisory board may depend on much or how little funding you have. With adequate funding, you can offer consulting fees. You will have to be more creative if you have only a small amount of (or no) funding to accomplish the goals of your project and support an advisory board (see Tips and Tactics in the feature box on the previous page). Locating funding sources and proposal writing are beyond the scope of this book.

Your advisory board should consist of persons with expertise in each of the areas pertinent to the success of the project. Let's imagine for a moment that your planned media project is a Web resource for children in primary grades. The overall purpose of that resource is to teach them Internet evaluation skills while naturally engaging them in the process. Who should be on your advisory board?

Start with persons who have content expertise in the area of evaluation, perhaps one or more individuals working in fields related to information literacy. Information literacy means being able to identify when information is needed and having the skills to locate, access, evaluate, and use that information. With a little luck, you may even be able to land the director of a prominent national information literacy organization. Don't become deflated if that person is too busy; she may be able to recommend others who would be perfect for your board. If your target audience includes children in the second and third grades, you will also want educators and parents. All have a perspective that you need to hear. Even if your project staff includes top-notch Web designers, artists, and writers, you may still want to include a Web designer, writer, or other creative types on your advisory board to expand your creative resources.

How large you make your advisory board involves both budgetary and management considerations. If you physically convene at a location, you will

THE CTW MODEL 15

have some cash outlays for supplying snacks, lunches, and so on. The more members you have on the board and the more often you meet, the more managing is required—planning, arrangements, follow-up, and so on.

Educators and scholars resent being called on to rubber-stamp a project. If you are serious about developing quality children's media, you will sincerely want their opinions and ideas. Many educators can provide excellent input for the creative implementation of a goal.

Prioritizing Curriculum Goals and Objectives

The result of the efforts of the production experts and educators on the advisory board is a prioritized list of curriculum goals and objectives compiled into a concept paper with summaries of the literature in the field. This becomes an important document for your project team as a guide and reference.

Your goals will broadly identify the areas your project will address. There may be as many as five or six or as few as one or two (if, for example, you are producing a single video, software product, print piece, etc.).

Let's return to the example of the Web evaluation resource for children in the second and third grades. On the broadest level, the project goal might be: The child can evaluate resources. Subsumed under that would likely be several subgoals under different headings such as "Print Resources" and "Internet Resources." These goals would be sequenced so that the child would first be taught to use evaluation skills with more familiar resources such as books and print, moving later to the Internet.

Broad goals and subgoals identify generally what the child will do or know in various categories that may relate to knowledge, skills, attitudes, or procedures. Your project has the greatest chance of succeeding when your goals are clarified as specific and measurable instructional objectives.

In the evaluation resource example, there would be goals related to the various attributes of evaluation, including accuracy, credibility (including authority), currency, comprehensiveness, and so on. Let's focus on credibility.

For this age-group, credibility would be replaced by words such as "true" or "factual." Here is an example of a general goal with one of several possible specific objectives:

Goal: The child will be able to judge whether a website seems true (credible).

Objective: Given a page from a bogus website with obvious exaggerations, the third-grade child can identify three out of five clues that the page represents false or inaccurate information.

If your project is Web based, a video or television series, or other media without a stipulated end date, expect your goals and objectives to expand and evolve over time.

Be As Specific As Possible!

The specificity of your objectives will determine how easy or difficult it will later be to measure the outcome of your media project. Try to be as specific as possible. However, not every goal and objective will be easily measured quantitatively, especially some social and affective goals. In those cases, you may need to consider some of the rich ways of collecting data, qualitatively such as observation, interviews, and case studies.

The Writer's Notebook

Educators and media people have their own jargon. One in the presence of the other might even say they speak different languages, when talking on a topic of their expertise. The Writer's Notebook at CTW was used to help producers conceptualize the curriculum goals and objectives in plain English, and translate them into producible segments that would engage the audience. Educators would think of potential ways to demonstrate a concept, for example, often coming up with creative suggestions. This might be enough to both clarify the objective and get the creative juices flowing for the production team. The Writer's Notebook also included general guidelines.

THE CTW MODEL

The Writer's Notebook was useful on several of my projects and occasionally included expanded treatment ideas suggested by advisers inclined to test their creative skills. Some were used, while others were modified or not used at all. I found it helpful to include background material on the topic or concept. Some writers appreciate the extra material. Others may find it distracting. You will have to experiment to see what works best with your team.

Production Research and Production (or Development)

CTW has historically allocated a portion of its program budgets to develop test shows. A distinction is made between "test" shows and "pilot" shows because pilot shows generally end up being broadcast. The test shows, on the other hand, were not mandated for airing. The test shows allowed the production staff to test out a variety of ideas to see if they worked pedagogically and creatively with the target audience without worrying about broadcast. It allowed the CTW production staff to stretch more than they might have with the broadcast restrictions.

Big-budget projects can afford the luxury of test shows. Ideally all projects would include this effort. However, that is not always feasible. Even if you cannot create entire test shows (or test websites, videos, or magazines), you may be able to economically test certain program features that could impact your media project in some way. It might be a particular segment idea or even a production effect that helps signal children to attend to a certain part of the screen, for example. Whatever additional information you have on what works and doesn't work with your audience helps you to move closer to achieving your project goals.

If your project is Web based or software based (as opposed to television or video), you will likely refer to the production phase as "development" and to production research as your "prototype." I am currently working on a Web-based project that is in the development stage. Prior to development, our project team created a working prototype that included much of the planned functionality of the end product, without the bells and whistles. This project, called S.O.S. for Information Literacy, is actually targeted for educators of K–8 students but includes materials they would use with this group. I mention this project because it exemplifies the importance of production research or, in this case, developing a prototype. Prior to developing a prototype, we had done a front-end analysis that included a thorough library review, as well as surveys and interviews with members of our target audience. We thought we knew what they wanted, and, for the most part, we were on track. However, without the feedback and recommendations the project team received once potential users had the opportunity to actually interact with a prototype, we might have produced a product that our target audience would fail to adopt. The testing of the prototype resulted in numerous modifications and additions. We conducted the testing of our prototype with online focus groups interacting asynchronously with others in the group and with staff. We set up several different discussion "threads" addressing a number of both content and functionality issues.

Online Focus Groups

There is a certain dynamic that can take place when six to ten children are in a conference room during a facilitated focus group. However, there are times when this may not be feasible. With older children, an alternative might be an online focus group, especially if your product is Web based. Online focus groups also remove geographic barriers to participation.

Just as production research helps inform decisions before full-scale production begins, the actual production becomes the focus of a research effort that is constantly informing new production decisions. This is called formative research or formative evaluation, the topic of the next section.

Formative and Summative Research/Evaluation

One of the cornerstones of the CTW model is the comprehensive formative and summative research that is connected with each program effort. At the end of this chapter, I suggest a recent publication that covers thirty years of research on children and *Sesame Street* alone. For students of television, film, and video, this would be an excellent addition to your media research collection. It includes two chapters dedicated to exploring the role and issues related to formative research. If you want a book dedicated to formative evaluation only, I suggest Barbara Flagg's volume listed at the end of the chapter.

In the next few paragraphs, I will give you a brief introduction to the important role that research plays in media projects. First, we need to distinguish between formative and summative research. They serve quite different purposes.

Formative research is intended to help inform production decisions during the production of a series. It is as relevant to Web-based and interactive technologies as it is to television. Often formative research (sometimes called evaluation) is conducted in-house with research staff. While this may not sound as rigorous and unbiased as research conducted by outside sources, the research is no less serious; the success of the project depends on informed decision making. Its purpose is to help the writers and producers understand if what they are creating works with the target audience before the entire series (or individual episode in many cases) is produced, the budget exhausted, and the results disappointing. To be meaningful, formative research should be conducted with scholarly attention to issues concerning subject selection, methodology, and analysis.

Formative research can be used to test a number of production issues such as viewer (television/video) or user (Web and other new media) comprehension of content presented, appeal factors, attitudinal change, and recall and/or retention of facts. Perhaps you have added a new character to your media project. How well is the character being received by children and do different children (e.g., sex, race, age) relate differently to the character? Before entering into a long-term contract with a talent, you might want to do some testing. You could also use formative research for something as simple as a new production effect used as a transition between segments. Do children understand this as a transition or is it confusing?

Observations, one-on-one interviews, and parent surveys are formative research methods you could employ. CTW developed a number of innovative techniques for gathering data, including eye-movement photography to determine where on the television screen the child's eyes were focused at different times. You might use a technique like this to decide where to position the salient aspects of the screen. It was used by researcher Barbara Flagg, for example, during the production of *The Electric Company*.

One component of the formative evaluation effort of the Web-based project described earlier is what we termed a "progressive feedback panel." Its purpose is to periodically review development efforts as new functionality and features are added to the resource. This group is called progressive because these individuals from the target audience will stay with us throughout the eighteen-month development phase and provide ongoing feedback. Members are paid a modest honorarium for their services and enjoy functioning as part of a development effort.

While the primary goal of formative research is to guide programming decisions during production, the goal of summative research is to assess the impact of a program on the intended audience after the fact. Frequently summative research or what is more often referred to as summative evaluation is conducted by an outside service to avoid the slightest possibility of researcher bias.

Since summative evaluations are concerned with whether a program has achieved its stated objectives, measures of the study participants' knowledge, skills, and attitudes are generally taken before exposure to the program and then measured afterward. Naturally, one hopes that the audience has made significant gains in the areas that the project's curriculum addressed as compared with results of those who did not participate in the program. Researchers also look for other intervening variables that might have influenced the audience's gain or lack of gain in the areas of interest.

Summative evaluations are useful for proving to funders that your media project worked (or, ouch, didn't). They may also help procure follow-on funding or funding for a related project, if your outcome was successful.

FINAL NOTE

There are many evaluation models you can use with your project. For example, Web-based projects may employ what is sometimes called user-based or user-centered evaluation. As its name implies, it considers the user in the actual design phase of the product. Many of what are referred to as "models" may, in fact, be more like evaluation "techniques" that can be subsumed under the larger umbrella of formative evaluation. So, please become familiar with as many models or techniques as may be appropriate for your project but realize that the bottom line is that you have a good way of informing your production/development decisions along the way to your final product.

In recent years, outcome-based evaluation (OBE) has been used by educational and governmental agencies as a systematic approach to determining the extent to which a program has achieved its stated goals. OBE could easily be applied to children's media projects with specific learning goals. You can find out more about OBE by conducting a simple online search.

THE CTW MODEL

COMING UP NEXT...

This chapter was designed to give you some background on the CTW model and some ideas for how you might implement it in your own projects. It is a proven model that provides a systematic way to develop your media project. Addressing motivation is also important. Although all CTW program offerings across all media incorporate motivational strategies, the next chapter will introduce you to a wonderful model that provides a systematic framework for addressing motivation in every one of your projects. Then chapter 4 brings together the CTW model with the ARCS model in a powerful combination.

PRODUCER'S CHECKLIST

Using the CTW (now Sesame Workshop) approach to producing children's media projects, the following are important ingredients for a successful outcome:

- ❏ Solid preliminary research on your project idea and demonstration that it can address a significant need.
- ❏ An advisory board whose members have expertise in all areas of importance to the project from educators to producers (and the ability to work well together).
- ❏ Clear curriculum goals and specific measurable objectives.
- ❏ A means of clarifying educational objectives for production staff without jargon, and with possible ideas for addressing those objectives (e.g., Writer's Notebook).
- ❏ Production research before actual production begins such as test programs, test segments, and so on.
- ❏ Formative research during media production to inform and guide decision making while there is still time to make changes in your media product.
- ❏ Summative evaluation to assess how well your project achieved its goals with your target audience.

DIGGING DEEPER

To learn more about the CTW model, the formative and summative research conducted for its programs, and research in interactive technologies, consider the following books and articles.

"Children's Learning from Television: Research and Development at the Children's Television Workshop." *Educational Technology Research and Development* 38, no. 4 (1990).

Fisch, Shalom M., and Truglio, Rosemarie T., eds. 2001. *"G" is for Growing: Thirty Years of Research on Children and Sesame Street.* Mahwah, N.J.: Erlbaum.

Flagg, Barbara N., ed. 1990. *Formative Evaluation for Educational Technology.* Hillsdale, N.J.: Erlbaum.

Lesser, Gerald S. 1974. *Children and Television: Lessons from Sesame Street.* New York: Vintage.

Palmer, Edward L. 1988. *Television and America's Children: A Crisis of Neglect.* New York: Oxford University Press.

THE ARCS MODEL

The ARCS model of motivational design was developed by Professor John Keller of Florida State University. His model has been used extensively in this country and abroad (particularly in Japan) in the motivational design and redesign of educational materials. I discovered the model during my studies at Syracuse University as a doctoral student in instructional design, development, and evaluation. Ruth Small, one of my professors, dubbed students who had internalized the model "ARCS angels." I soon realized the strength and practicality of the model and became an ARCS angel myself! You will find this model to be a heuristic, easy-to-apply approach for developing the motivational design of your media projects.

The ARCS model is used in tandem with the instructional design process. Instructional design is a process used by educators and developers to decide what methods are best suited to teach which content to what audience under which conditions. (I can just hear the communication students reading this chapter saying "Huh?" You are right. This is a bit of educational jargon.) Time for a Take 2!

What Is Instructional Design?

Instructional design means determining the best methods of presenting instruction so that learning occurs. It involves identifying specific learning goals and planning what methods to use to teach the knowledge, skills, procedures, and so on, necessary to achieve specific goals.

Keller began to work on motivation and learning in the late 1970s. He believed that not all the variation in achievement among learners could be attributed to ability alone. Some of what contributed to differences had to be credited to effort. There is tremendous variability among learners with respect to how much effort they apply in a learning situation. A number of variables factor into effort (e.g., cognitive, social, behavioral, and learning style variables), plus those associated with the design of the instructional materials themselves. All of these have a motivational impact on the learner, affecting subsequent effort and helping to account for some of the differences among learners in achievement.

Keller's model maintains that the process of designing instruction (developing curriculum goals and objectives, evaluating, etc.) should include the same rigor in designing motivational goals as it does for designing its instructional or learning goals. Yet Keller's model is one of the only comprehensive, theory-based models that offers a process for both determining what the motivational goals should be and prescribing strategies for their attainment. If you do not achieve your motivational goals, your audience probably won't learn or accept the content you produce. In chapter 1, I pointed out that without value and an expectation for success, it is unlikely that learners will be motivated. The ARCS model incorporates many powerful motivation theories and constructs, but underlying it all is expectancy-value theory. Briefly, I will present the theoretical underpinnings of the model.

THEORETICAL BASIS FOR THE ARCS MODEL

What accounts for the stimulation, direction, intensity, and persistence of behavior? Motivation. In chapter 1, you learned that motivation is best measured by effort. In the following I expand on that notion.

Keller and others make a distinction between effort and performance as categories of behavior. Performance refers to accomplishing a goal relative to a set standard, and thus it is measured against the standard. Performance can be influenced by factors such as ability or skill and is fairly easy to measure. Effort refers to engaging in endeavors with the intent to achieve a goal. It is usually measured by the persistence or the intensity of the effort. A common measure is "time on task"—how long does the child try to achieve the desired behavior, skill, or knowledge? It is not necessarily related to ability. Thus effort can be considered a direct measure of motivation. Since performance can be affected by ability or other factors, it is considered an indirect measure.

The ARCS model is based on expectancy-value theory, and this framework allows us to examine other theories that factor into both value and expectancy for success. Let's start with value.

Value

Value, relevance, meaningfulness. These terms could easily be used interchangeably in discussing the value component of E-V theory. Yet what creates value? A number of theories and motivational principles relate to this component. This book is practical and not intended to be overly burdensome with theories, yet there is one that I would like to briefly mention here, as you may readily see how it applies even to yourself.

David McClelland, who wrote *The Achieving Society*, described several human motives based on needs: (1) the need for achievement (a need to attain a level of personal excellence, (2) the need for affiliation (a need to find opportunities for social interaction), and (3) the need for power (a need to have an impact on others). While all of us may have all these needs to some extent, his theory holds that individuals are strongest in one of the three and less so in the other two. (Although need for power is sometimes thought of negatively, it can be good if used for the benefit of others. Many of our present and former great leaders were high in need for power.) Which need is highest for you?

There are other need theories that affect value, such as Abraham Maslow's famous hierarchy of needs. Theories on curiosity, flow, and numerous others also relate to value. We will see how in later chapters.

EXPECTANCY FOR SUCCESS (OR EXPECTATION FOR SUCCESS)

As mentioned in chapter 1, expectation for success is based on the child's perception of his or her success potential for achieving a goal, if attempted.

Again, there are numerous theories that relate to expectancy for success. For example, attribution theory refers to how people explain their successes and failures. A child who feels she has little or no control over her circumstances will attribute her outcomes to external factors such as task difficulty or luck. A child with an internal orientation who succeeds on a task may attribute the success to ability or effort.

Have you ever heard a child exclaim something like, "I just can't do it. I'm not smart enough and I won't try!" The child may believe that statement because of past experiences and failures. This is called learned helplessness and would obviously influence expectation for success. In part 2 of this book, you'll discover strategies you can employ in your media projects that will address these and other motivational constructs.

Remember there is a multiplicative function between value and expectation for success. If either of these factors is missing (zero), the individual will not be motivated.

Now that you have the foundation for the model, you will easily see how the four components of the ARCS model fit in this theoretical framework. Have you been wondering what the acronym ARCS stands for? Read on.

Developmental Snapshot
The Child at Five

By five years of age, most children are far less demanding of their parents and their social behavior has much improved. They have also advanced a good deal in their physical coordination. They have much more control and persist at tasks for long periods of time. They strive for accuracy as they attempt to draw and write, and this helps them improve their manual dexterity in preparation for school. Rather than "Why this?" and "Why that?" questions of the four-year-old, five-year-olds are likely to ask more directed questions, which are easier for the adults in their lives to answer.

Their apparent self-sufficiency is a joy to watch. ("The Child at Six" is in Chapter 4.)

Note: Developmental snapshots are necessarily general and do not take into consideration wide variations in individual differences related to personality, learning, or physical development.

COMPONENTS OF THE MODEL

ARCS stands for:

- Attention
- Relevance
- Confidence
- Satisfaction

According to this model, the items listed previously represent the four areas that must be addressed to motivate learning. (In part 2, you will discover dozens of strategies that you can incorporate into your media projects to gain and sustain attention, create relevance, and build confidence and satisfaction.) Can you see how these four requirements relate to expectancy-value theory?

Attention and relevance relate to the "value" component while confidence and satisfaction are associated with "expectancy for success" (see figure 2). You must get your learner's attention and then, even more challenging, sustain it. You must connect with what is important, interesting, or meaningful to establish relevance. If you accomplish these things, you have value. That is a good start but you are still only halfway there. Your learners must also have confidence they can do what you are asking. It is up to you to find ways to help them succeed and to feel responsible for their outcomes. Finally, your product should instill in your viewers/users a continuing motivation to

VALUE		EXPECTANCY for SUCCESS	
Attention	Relevance	Confidence	Satisfaction

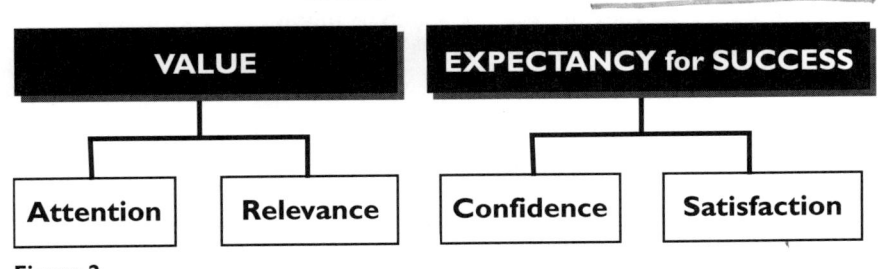

Figure 2.

learn—the satisfaction component. Perhaps you reinforce success with a reward of some kind that taps into their intrinsic motivation. When you have successfully addressed both confidence and satisfaction, you have created an expectation for success.

Each component in figure 2 will be explored in separate chapters to identify motivational strategies that will work for your media project.

PROCESS OF MOTIVATIONAL DESIGN

Keller delineates several phases in the motivational design process, each with associated activities. In this chapter, you will be introduced to the process. In the next chapter, we will walk through the process with an example.

Audience Motivational Analysis

By conducting an audience analysis, you will gain an understanding of both situational and audience characteristics—variables that may impact children's motivation to learn from or participate in your media-based project. How might you begin such an analysis?

One way is to access historical data or typical profiles for your audience. If possible, it means interacting with or observing members of your target audience to identify motivational gaps. In this way, you can adjust the model to adapt to the needs of your audience. You may need a few attention strategies, for example, whereas you may need more for creating relevance. There may be large confidence deficits due to past experiences, self-concept problems, and the like. Or there may an overconfidence problem that also leads to poor performance.

Let's assume you are producing a video to teach seven- and eight-year-olds about the topic of weather, a science-related topic. Along with the video, you are preparing a print support piece to reinforce and expand on the learning from the video. Your motivational analysis might begin with doing basic library research about children and science instruction. One of the first things you discover is that girls are somewhat less scientifically inclined than boys. Why is that? Several resources you reviewed mentioned that girls often don't think they are as good at science as boys. Another mentioned that boys are more often positively reinforced for displaying scientific knowledge than girls, and so on. Hmm. Sounds like you may need to address confidence for the females in your audience. You might also interview a few classroom teachers who teach the topic; you are likely to discover that students don't find this topic exciting. Some call it "boring. All I have to do is look out the window. If it's raining, I put on my raincoat." What's going on here? The students are not interested in the topic because they don't see the value in learning about it. You'll have to do something about that! These are just a couple of examples of how you might begin to analyze your audience.

Once you have reviewed all the information you have garnered, you can create a motivational profile. Your motivational profile is the crucial first step in the motivational design process. Using the previous example, you will have to concentrate on creating value for all students and confidence, in particular, for females. Using the results of your profile, you can establish your motivational objectives.

Motivational Objectives

Your audience motivational analysis has identified the potential motivational deficits of your target audience. You have a basic idea of the motivational dynamics and thus where you should focus your efforts. Unlike instructional objectives that are specific (see chapter 2), your motivational objectives are, by design, somewhat broader. Using the weather topic example from the previous section, let's look at a few appropriate motivational objectives. Remember, our motivational profile indicated we would need to focus on creating relevance and building confidence. So, more objectives would be expected for those categories, although we would not want to overlook the general importance of gaining and sustaining attention or of providing satisfaction.

Attention	Viewers will demonstrate curiosity about the weather.
Relevance	Viewers will recognize how the weather has affected them in the past.
	Viewers will see how understanding the weather can be of value to them in the future.
	Viewers will select a follow-up project that suits their learning preferences.
Confidence	Viewers, and in particular girls, will realize that their success on the weather topic is based on both their efforts and abilities.
	Viewers clearly understand the learning objectives of the video.
	Viewers understand what is expected of them as a result of watching the video.

	Viewers will demonstrate a positive expectation that they can demonstrate what they have learned from the video.
Satisfaction	Viewers will want to know more about the weather.

Designing Strategies

Now comes the fun part! The three steps are (1) brainstorming, (2) selection, and (3) sequencing. I will give you a taste of this process here, and we'll do lots more in chapters 5–8.

Step 1 Brainstorm as many strategies as you can think of that could possibly address each objective you have listed. Get others who understand your motivation objectives to help you. The purpose here is idea generation—not selection. That will come next. Do not limit your creativity or put too many constraints on your brainstorming team. Come up with as many ideas as you can.

For attention, Keller suggests three main subcategories for designing strategies:

- Perceptual arousal (strategies to capture their interest)
- Inquiry arousal (strategies to stimulate an attitude of inquiry)
- Variability (strategies to sustain their attention)

Continuing with our weather example and our single attention objective, you would be most interested in inquiry arousal. One strategy for that is to stimulate curiosity. Perhaps you could do that in the opening of your video.

Strategy applied to video example: Video fades up on a close-up of a leaf. It moves and the camera follows it. Then we cut to a wider shot that shows trees bending in the wind and leaves blowing all around. An unseen child with an inquisitive-sounding voice makes a statement followed by a question: "Wind can move leaves and objects like chairs. But have you ever wondered what moves wind?"

We had more objectives for relevance, so you need to brainstorm more strategies for that category. The subcategories for relevance are:

- Goal orientation (strategies that meet the learners' needs)
- Motive matching (strategies that address students' personal interests, learning styles, or personality characteristics)
- Familiarity (strategies that build on learners' personal experiences)

Our objective—viewers will see how understanding the weather can be of value to them in the future—mostly relates to goal orientation (future worth).

The strategy of showing the benefit of learning the weather concepts could be exemplified in the following way:

Strategy applied to video example: Fade up on scene showing kids planning an outdoor event for the next day. They predict a thunderstorm based on their observations and knowledge of how heat, air, and water combine in different ways. They adjust their plans to account for this contingency. One child exclaims, "It's cool to know about weather!"

This strategy demonstrates the utility of the knowledge by selecting an event with perceived relevance to the on-screen children. We enhanced the basic strategy by having one of the children model excitement for learning about the topic. Modeling increases its relevance because a child with whom the audience can identify made the statement. Remember, the motivational strategy is integrated with content that has been designed to address the curriculum or instructional objective.

By now, you should be getting the idea of how motivational strategies relate to the motivational objectives and how your objectives were driven by your audience motivational analysis. Let me give you the subcategories associated with confidence and satisfaction before moving along.

The confidence subcategories are:

- Learning requirements (strategies that help learners build a positive expectation for success)
- Success opportunities (strategies that support learners' perceived competence)
- Personal responsibility (strategies that help learners understand that their success is based on effort as well as ability)

The subcategories associated with satisfaction are:

- Intrinsic reinforcement (strategies that encourage learners' intrinsic motivation to learn)
- Extrinsic rewards (strategies that provide appropriate rewards for success)
- Equity (strategies that let the learner know he or she is being treated fairly)

Step 2 Once you have a good list of strategies, you can pick and choose the best ones for each objective. Now is the time to be selective. You must consider both your resources (including budget) and the time you expect to have with your target audience for this. A half-hour video, for example, will put constraints on the number of strategies you can incorporate, and, according to your analysis, you must focus on some more than others.

Step 3 Finally you must decide on an appropriate sequence for your strategies. The attention strategy mentioned earlier was obviously intended to be at the beginning of the video. When should your relevance strategies be used? Perhaps one of them should come early on in the video in order for your audience to buy into your topic. Then sprinkle one or more throughout the body of your video along with your confidence strategies. Your satisfaction strategy might best be saved for the ending section of the video.

All your motivational strategies must be integrated with the actual curriculum content. (To review curriculum objectives, see chapter 2.)

Developing Your Strategies

This step dovetails with production in the CTW model, and I will bring these two together in the next chapter.

Evaluate (or Pilot-Test)

Just as you must evaluate whether you have achieved your instructional objectives, you must also know if you have achieved success from a motivational perspective. What should you measure and how should you do it? Think back to your motivational objectives; these should help dictate your motivational measures. Just as motivational objectives are fuzzier than instructional objectives, so are the measures. Let's refer back to the weather video example. What might possibly be some of the measures? Here are a few suggestions:

- Use observation. Observe males and females as they watch your video. Note their reactions, for example, to the attention strategy you used to open the video and others throughout. You could observe individually or in a group situation. Pay special attention to both verbal and nonverbal cues such as facial expressions, physical movements, and so on.
- Convene a focus group that includes both males and females. Develop a protocol that could be followed by an impartial facilitator. Find out what was relevant to them. Ask special questions of the girls to see if they feel confident about the material.

THE ARCS MODEL

- Do a comparative analysis. Compare a group of learners who have not seen the video with those who have on both motivation and a test of achievement. Compare scores overall. Then look at just the girls. Did girls who viewed the video score higher on the test than girls who did not view the video (we planned on incorporating strategies to bolster confidence in females)? If you have no research experience, ask a research expert to help you design a measure of this complexity. Remember that achievement or actual performance is an indirect measure of motivation. The next one is a direct measure.
- Measure time on task. With the same group of participants as described previously, measure how long each group persists on answering the questions posed on the achievement test. For this to work, the test must not have a time limit. Persistence is a measure of effort, and effort is directly related to motivation!

These are just a few possible measures. What others can you think of that could help measure the motivational objectives?

Watch Out!

When observing children, try not to be overly intrusive as they could miss valuable content or become too self-conscious.

FINAL NOTE

It is not possible to incorporate enough strategies to meet every learner's needs and personal preferences. Do try to address a range of individual differences by at least incorporating strategies that will motivate as many different learners as is feasible with your production.

If you have any doubt that Keller's model has made a tremendous impact on people like you and me who are interested in the design of motivating learning materials, do a simple Google search. Type in "+ARCS +Model" and I guarantee you will get more than 200,000 hits!

COMING UP NEXT ...

The next chapter brings together the CTW model and the ARCS model for a powerful systematic approach to designing media for children!

PRODUCER'S CHECKLIST

❏ The ARCS model of motivational design was developed by Florida State University professor John Keller and is the most widely used motivation model by educators.
❏ The ARCS model is designed to be used in tandem with the design and development of content/curriculum goals and objectives.
❏ The ARCS model is grounded in expectancy-value theory. According to E-V theory, one must both value a task and expect to be successful at it to be motivated. These notions are especially useful in designing media for children.
❏ A number of theories and motivational principles can be related to expectancy-value theory.
❏ The four components of the ARCS model are attention, relevance, confidence, and satisfaction.
❏ Attention and relevance relate to value. Confidence and satisfaction relate to expectancy for success.
❏ The process for designing motivation involves:
  • Audience motivational analysis
  • Motivational objectives
  • Designing strategies
  • Developing strategies
  • Evaluation

DIGGING DEEPER

If you would like to read more about John Keller's work, consult the following references, from most to least recent.

Keller, John M. 1999. "Motivation in Cyber Learning Environments." *International Journal of Educational Technology* 1, no. 1: 7–30. ERIC Digest, EJ611608.
Small, Ruth V. 1997. *Motivation in Instructional Design*. ERIC Digest, ED409895. www.ericfacility.net/databases/ERIC_Digests/ed409895.html.

Arnone, M. P., and Small, Ruth V. 1995. *Arousing and Sustaining Curiosity: Lessons from the ARCS Model.* ERIC Digest, ED383285.

Keller, J. M., and Keller, B. H. 1989. *Motivational Delivery Checklist.* Florida State University.

Keller, J. M., and Suzuki, K. 1988. "Use of the ARCS Motivation Model in Courseware Design." In D. H. Jonassen, ed., *Instructional Designs for Microcomputer Courseware.* Hillsdale, N.J.: Erlbaum.

Keller, J. M. 1987a. "Strategies for Stimulating the Motivation to Learn." *Performance and Instruction* 26, no. 8, 1–7.

Keller, J. M. 1987b. *IMMS: Instructional Materials Motivation Survey.* Florida State University.

Keller, J. M. 1983. "Motivational Design of Instruction." In C. M. Reigeluth, ed., *Instructional Design Theories and Models: An Overview of Their Current Status.* Hillsdale, N.J.: Erlbaum.

ADDITIONAL REFERENCE

McClelland, David. 1961. *The Achieving Society.* Princeton, N.J.: Van Nostrand.

4

AN INTEGRATIVE AND SYSTEMATIC APPROACH

Whether your project involves children navigating a website or viewing a television program, you need to be concerned with how your users or viewers feel about their experience, how you plan to create relevance, build their confidence, and provide satisfaction. Such motivational concerns are often handled intuitively by a producer or creative staff, without the same discipline that goes into the actual educational content. Yet success in meeting learning goals is almost always related to motivation. Additionally, motivation determines whether your target audience will come back for more—watch your program again or revisit your website. This chapter brings together the ARCS model and CTW model to provide producers a more systematic approach to handling motivation in educational children's media projects.

You will recall from the previous chapter that motivational design is conducted in tandem with the development of the specific content of your media project. This chapter brings these two powerful models together in a way that will help guide you through the process of producing media, whether you are developing a single media product that will support a larger curriculum or a series of videos, television programs, or an educational website.

First, a disclaimer. This book is not about video production techniques, software development, Web or multimedia design. Each specialty has its own development language and unique processes. (The use of the word "development" here is an umbrella term for all aspects of a project from beginning to end.) This book is about motivation and how it can be systematically integrated into a development model that considers the careful design of educational objectives. Because the CTW model is tailored specifically for children's media development, it provides an excellent scaffolding for the overlay of motivational design in media produced for the child audience. Yet I do not exhaustively describe every aspect of what goes into the production component or any other aspect of that model because the focus of this book is motivation.

That said, I would now like to bring these models together using five very general steps undertaken in almost any project, regardless of media type. As each of these steps is graphically depicted in the concept map and later discussed, you will clearly see how the CTW model and the ARCS model are totally compatible. These general steps are the following:

1. Front-end analysis
2. Content goals and objectives
3. Design
4. Production/development
5. Evaluation

You should also be able to envision, within the broadly defined steps, the unique tasks associated with the particular medium in which you are developing your project.

Notice that in the concept map shown in figure 3, the advisory board and Writer's Notebook, cornerstones of the CTW model, are now incorporated into the overall process.

FRONT-END ANALYSIS

Most development models, whether for television, Web, multimedia, or any of the new media, advocate a thorough front-end assessment or analysis. The needs of the target audience are analyzed and thus the necessity for the project is validated. The scope and vision of the project are defined and the overall project goals are articulated. This is consistent with the CTW model. Many commercial ventures also include a research or marketing analysis component at this stage to determine if there is really a potential audience for the media product. Methods range from interviews, surveys, and experimental design to focus groups, both in person and online. A development team is assembled and the various roles are determined including the de-

AN INTEGRATIVE AND SYSTEMATIC APPROACH

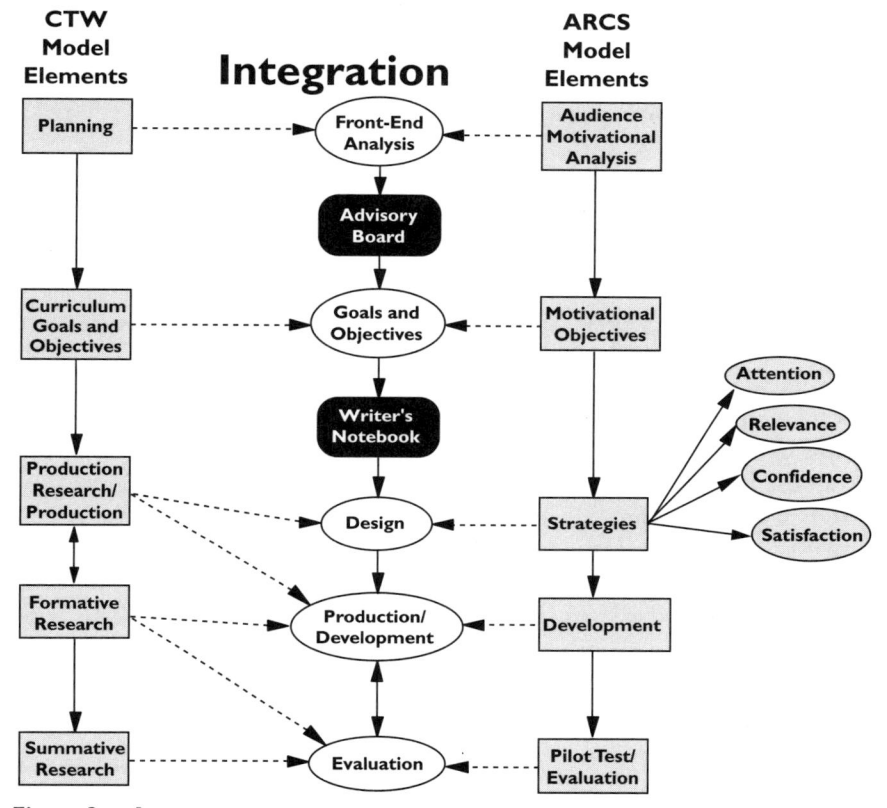

Figure 3. A concept map

sign and creative teams, and management. On small projects, one person may wear several hats.

The many aspects of planning on the CTW side and the audience motivational analysis on the ARCS side are merged in this critical first phase. Whatever label is given to this phase, it is an important first step in which all members of the project team must get onto the same page. Now that you have a plan of attack, you can move to the design stage.

CONTENT GOALS AND OBJECTIVES

Once the project team has agreed on the scope and direction of the project, specific objectives related to curriculum content can be identified. They almost always include learning objectives related to, for example,

- Concepts and principles
- Skills
- Procedural knowledge
- Attitudes and behavior

As noted in previous chapters, objectives must be measurable so that you can determine how effective your project was in achieving its desired outcomes. How will you know if the viewer or user has learned the concepts, skills, or procedures? Developing criterion measures of performance goes hand in hand with developing content goals and objectives.

Developing learning objectives requires an understanding of the developmental and experiential level of the target audience. Child development experts and subject matter experts (SMEs) working with producers to delineate doable objectives is one of the strengths of the CTW model. It is within the context of developing these specific learning objectives that motivational objectives are also addressed, along with their associated criterion measures for later evaluation.

As can be seen in the concept map showing the integration of the models, the advisory board, a hallmark of the CTW model, is placed to both serve the development of curriculum objectives on one side and motivational objectives on the other. Obviously the advisory board will include experts in motivation.

DESIGN

The design phase varies greatly depending on the type of project—television or video, multimedia, Web based, and so on. For example, a children's multimedia or Web-based project will include a number of design considerations that may not be tackled in the same way in a television or video project that is linear (sequential). Information design (the way the content is organized), interface design (how the user interacts with the system including the look and feel of the program), integration of links, and search mechanisms are all critical issues in the former. Information design and interface design are concepts that should also be considered in a linear medium. There is a lot of overlap. Anyone who produces projects for children, regardless of the media, must be concerned with graphics, video, sound, animation, and usually talent. Storyboarding, scripting, flowcharting, and numerous other tasks all converge during the design phase. Often a prototype, pilot, or working example is developed for initial testing of the appeal and effectiveness of the various elements. Production research, which for CTW includes producing complete test shows, feeds into the design phase of the concept map (as well as production/development). Also contributing to the design are motivational strategies to gain and maintain attention, create relevance, build confidence, and provide satisfaction and a continuing motivation to learn.

All design issues basically relate to how the children's media producer will handle the content of the media product. Whether the content is educational, purely entertainment, or what is most in demand today—content that is both educational and entertaining—the decisions made in the design phase are critical to the success of the project.

Notice in the concept map that the Writer's Notebook, a CTW trademark, also plays an important role in prescribing motivational input to the design team.

PRODUCTION/DEVELOPMENT

In this phase, all design decisions and specifications are transformed into reality, a product. If previous phases have been methodically executed, the production stage should go a lot more smoothly. I say "more smoothly" because we all know that things often don't go exactly to plan. There is always an element of uncertainty involved; if you can embrace that concept and realize that often the most creative solutions arise when you are open to uncertainty, you will sometimes achieve a better product than the one you initially conceived.

In the concept map, you can see that formative research (which may also include more production research) feeds production/development. The CTW model includes an ongoing relationship between production and formative research as indicated by the double arrows. On the ARCS model side, the realization of motivational strategies (development) occurs in this phase, as media is produced and strategies are embedded within media content.

Even though referred to as the development or production phase, it can usually be broken into several subphases. For example, what is generically referred to as "video production" is actually preproduction, production, and postproduction.

! Tips and Tactics

Thorough Preproduction Saves Dollars

The more time and effort you put into preproduction, the more time you will save during actual production. Production is expensive and time means money!

During preproduction the design specs are interpreted in terms of actual production needs. Production tasks must be broken down, a timeline for completion established, a production plan created, and individuals assigned specific production elements. Readers who are video producers know that these elements include production design, graphics production, animation, videography, music and audio production, just to name a few. Someone may be engaged in gathering existing elements that can be repurposed for the new project. And copyright issues must then be explored and resolved. Although some functions must precede others, the work is not necessarily carried out in a linear fashion. Several individuals or teams can be working on one task while others are working simultaneously on another. To keep this all straight, often a simplified version of a PERT or Gantt chart (ways of tracking tasks, time, and costs on a project) is used. Most producers I know have their own way of tracking that works for them. Talent is usually cast during preproduction. As producer, you have a lot of things to juggle from hiring or coordinating your team to staying on top of allocated budget items, including time estimates for completion of tasks.

Next up in our video production example is the actual production. This can occur in a studio or in the field. Camera operators, teleprompter personnel, audio technicians, lighting director, technical director, grips, director, and producer are either in the field or on the set. Talent must be coordinated and releases from parents of children involved in the production must be procured. Releases from adult talent must also be obtained. Children tire easily and their special needs must be addressed. They are alternately thirsty, hungry, tired, bored, and antsy, and sometimes downright uncooperative—especially if you are working with real kids (my preference) and not professionals. If they forget their lines or stumble, they can lose confidence. If they are there only because their parents want them to be "actors," they will not find this a personally meaningful experience. You will be happy to have some of the motivation strategies you'll discover in part 2 of this book in your repertoire to keep their attention, create relevance, and bolster their confidence, when necessary.

When all the elements are produced and/or gathered, they are brought together during postproduction. For a video or television program, it involves digitizing and editing all the elements, adding narration and music tracks, creating transitions often using sophisticated digital effects, incorporating any animations, and so on. This is accomplished in what is called on-line editing sessions. Usually, an off-line edit precedes an on-line edit as a way of assembling a kind of rough cut before spending big money in an on-line session. An EDL (edit decision list) is then compiled which is brought into the on-line session describing the clips, their length and placement (on the original media etc.). On the multimedia side, all this is presented to the programmers as individual files to be incorporated into the broader scope of a project that also is concerned with building an interface, search mechanisms, and so on.

EVALUATION

Formative evaluation (compare with evaluation in CTW model, chapter 2) helps guide decisions during development, while summative evaluation generally occurs at the end of a project to determine the extent to which the goals of the project were met. Outcome-based evaluation (OBE) is an alternative among other models that could be employed.

In the concept map, you can see how both formative and summative research (CTW side) and pilot test/evaluation (ARCS side) relate to the overall evaluation effort.

Evaluation is often needed when funding comes from a government source and/or when an end date for project completion is set. Often commercial projects such as a children's program, website, or series of multimedia materials do not have planned end dates and continue to conduct formative evaluation along the way to make improvements. Thus summative evaluation is not of great concern. Unfortunately many children's media projects have no planned evaluation components.

Developmental Snapshot
The Child at Six

By six years of age, children are entering what is often referred to as the "middle years" of childhood. The six-year-old is packed with energy and in constant motion as she explores her world. Her vitality can be a joy to behold, but watch out! That same energy can be channeled to physical and verbal aggressiveness. Watching her, you wonder what happened to the apparent poise of the five-year-old! She wants everything and wants it *now!* She can't understand why, when she perceives a need, her parents can't just drop everything and attend to it. The six-year-old's world revolves around her. She wants attention and will say what she has to in order to win her "best friend" of choice. She likes school and is making great learning strides especially in the area of reading. Yet it is not easy to stick with a task for long periods. When she accomplishes something, she loves to be recognized for it. With what you know so far about motivation, what might be some of the challenges you would face producing media for this age?

Note: Developmental snapshots are necessarily general and do not take into consideration wide variations in individual differences related to personality, learning, or physical development.

FINAL NOTE

Part 1 of this book has introduced you to the CTW and ARCS models, ending in this chapter's conceptualization of how you can integrate these models in the development process. Whatever specific development model you are currently employing, I hope you can readily envision how to incorporate the strengths of the models discussed and begin to systematically incorporate motivational design into your future projects.

COMING UP NEXT ...

Part 2 of this book focuses on theoretically sound yet practical motivational strategies for accomplishing your motivation goals. With its many examples,

AN INTEGRATIVE AND SYSTEMATIC APPROACH

you will find it a handy reference that you can use as a catalyst for brainstorming your own ideas for your next children's media project. Chapter 5 begins with attention strategies.

PRODUCER'S CHECKLIST

- ❏ Designing motivation into children's media has traditionally been handled by producers in an intuitive rather than systematic manner, yet motivation plays a key role in accomplishing learning objectives.
- ❏ Regardless of media type, five common steps in the development process are conducting a front-end analysis, determining goals and objectives, design, production/development, and evaluation. The two models (CTW and ARCS) fit well within this general framework.
- ❏ An integration of the CTW model and the ARCS model makes use of an advisory board to help in developing and prioritizing motivational goals in addition to content goals and objectives. Experts in motivation should participate on the board.
- ❏ The Writer's Notebook should include ideas for motivational strategies that support specific learning objectives.
- ❏ An evaluation effort must include assessing the effectiveness of the media product in achieving both its learning and motivational goals.

DIGGING DEEPER

References for both the CTW model and the ARCS model were suggested in chapters 2 and 3, respectively.

Part 2

MOTIVATIONAL STRATEGIES FOR CHILDREN'S MEDIA

5

GAINING AND SUSTAINING ATTENTION

Attention is the first component required to establish the value of your media project. There is probably more research on gaining and sustaining children's attention than any of the other motivation components. One of the best-known methods of studying attention was called the distractor technique used by Edward Palmer to determine children's attention to particular television program elements. As children watched a program, images were projected onto a screen in the same room at regular intervals, competing for their attention. In this way, researchers could note exactly when a child's attention was on the program and when attention waned, as indicated by looking at the distractor screen. In this chapter, you will learn many strategies you can use to capture and sustain children's attention and a few caveats, as well.

The Research Says...

Production features that hold children's visual attention include lively music, sound effects, and especially children's voices. However, long speeches, adult male voices, and long camera zooms result in decreased attention (Rice, Huston, and Wright 1983).

THE ATTENTION COMPONENT OF THE ARCS MODEL

The ARCS model includes three primary categories of strategies for gaining and sustaining attention:

- Perceptual arousal
- Inquiry arousal
- Variability

We will look at each of these individually and apply them to children's media.

PERCEPTUAL AROUSAL

Perceptual arousal can include any sensory stimulus that initially grabs a child's attention such as a loud noise or an abrupt transition from a soft piece of music to a loud or raucous-sounding piece. An abrupt change can stimulate perceptual curiosity but is not lasting. To engage the learner so that his curiosity persists requires inquiry arousal, which is discussed later in this chapter.

! **Tips and Tactics**

Strive for an Optimal Level!

Using strategies for stimulating perceptual arousal will help avoid potential boredom or lost interest by viewers/users. But remember the old saying, Everything in moderation. Strive for an optimal level of perceptual arousal that does not interfere with your message!

Strategies for Creating Perceptual Arousal

Here are several strategies that relate to perceptual arousal. While not all of them may be appropriate for your project, you may wish to consider one or more depending on the content and the age of your audience.

Strategy 1: Incongruity, novelty, uncertainty. An incongruous statement that presents the child with a conceptual conflict is often effective with older children and can also be used for inquiry arousal. This can be used at the beginning of a presentation to grab attention. A novel visual effect accompanied by an appropriate sound effect is frequently used in video and television programs to gain attention.

Strategy 2: Surprise. Videos and television programs have long incorporated the element of surprise when a program suddenly introduces an unexpected guest such as a celebrity. Film producers are great at incorporating surprise. How about that first shark sighting in *Jaws?* Audience members literally rose out of their seats! Introducing an unfamiliar object or element is also useful for inducing perceptual arousal. What other types of "surprises" might be appropriate for your project?

Strategy 3: Make the abstract concrete. This strategy focuses on older children, since you will have difficulty addressing anything of an abstract nature with very young children. Try talking about a faraway place like Egypt or Australia to a five- or six-year-old. Making the abstract more concrete is a way to increase perceptual arousal. For example, a child is more likely to attend to an explanation of a concept when it is visualized in some way, for example, a concept map, animation, cartoon, or dramatization. Also useful are anecdotes, analogies, and demonstrations. These elements also add variability, the third aspect of attention in the ARCS model.

Strategy 4: Humor. Humor can gain the attention of your audience, but the type of humor that is effective varies with age. For example, young children love to play with language as in learning new or big words, but they won't understand puns or plays on words. They find "banana peel" or physical humor appealing and exaggerated physical action amusing. Older children can appreciate more verbal types of humor.

Strategy 5: Music. A change in music can be used to signal attention to a new segment. It has also been found to be effective in regaining lost attention.

Watch Out!

Beware of the Talking Head!

This overused mode of presentation is a definite attention robber, especially when the talking head is an adult.

INQUIRY AROUSAL

How do you stimulate curiosity and an attitude of inquiry in a child? Since I believe inquiry arousal is the most important factor for maintaining and sustaining attention, we will spend some time on the concept of curiosity.

Background on Curiosity

While there are many ways to explain curiosity, any discussion of the topic must begin with Daniel Berlyne, considered the seminal mind in the field of curiosity. His neurophysiological view associated curiosity with exploratory behavior. He identified two forms of exploratory behavior, diversive (e.g., seeking relief from boredom) and specific (e.g., uncertainty, conceptual conflict). Specific curiosity is of greatest interest to media producers of educational materials. Berlyne described specific exploration in the context of epistemic curiosity, calling it "the brand of arousal that motivates the quest for knowledge and is relieved when knowledge is procured." It follows that epistemic curiosity results in specific exploration. This exploration ultimately resolves the uncertainty or conceptual conflict and returns the individual to a moderate, pleasurable tonus level. Although his work was cut short by his untimely death, his accomplishments paved the way for later investigations into the area of curiosity.

Berlyne's colleague, Hy Day, extended his work in the 1980s, representing it graphically as a curvilinear relationship between level of arousal (or stimulation) and efficiency. At the optimal level, a person enters the zone of curiosity, characterized by exploration, excitement, and interest. Below the optimal level, the individual is unmotivated, disinterested, and inefficient. Beyond the optimal level, the individual enters a zone of anxiety with resulting behaviors, including defensiveness, disinterest, avoidance, and inefficiency. What might influence movement into the latter zone? Possible factors include too much stimulation for the child to handle or the cognitive conflict that is too difficult for the child's developmental and experiential level. This curvilinear explanation of curiosity was also used in a number of later studies, including my own. Keeping children in the zone of curiosity and out of the zone of anxiety is an important consideration for those who design interactive learning materials for children. While curiosity is described here as an attention component, keeping children in the zone of curiosity may also depend on addressing the confidence component, the subject of chapter 7.

Take 2

What Is the Zone of Curiosity?

The zone of curiosity is a phrase coined by researcher Hy Day. A child enters this zone when the curiosity-provoking situation has just the right amount of uncertainty for the child to handle. The child's attention will be sustained as she is motivated to find the answer and resolve her curiosity.

A number of researchers have placed more weight on cognitive and information processing factors in explaining curiosity. In the mid-1990s, Loewenstein proposed an information gap theory of specific epistemic curiosity: a feeling of deprivation occurs when an individual becomes aware of a difference between what one knows and what one wants to know. Could this be applied to children as well as adults? From an intuitive perspective, I think so. How many times have you heard a child ask "But how can that be?" until he receives an acceptable answer from an adult. The child needs to resolve that information gap.

Maw and Maw conducted a number of studies with elementary school-age children resulting in an operationalized definition of curiosity that I find very useful: "curiosity is demonstrated by an elementary school child when he: 1) reacts positively to new, strange, incongruous, or mysterious elements in his environment by moving toward them, by exploring, or by manipulating them, 2) exhibits a need or a desire to know more about himself and/or his environment, 3) scans his surroundings seeking new experiences, and 4) persists in examining and exploring stimuli in order to know more about them." If you are looking for ways to measure whether your media product stimulates a child's curiosity, you might find this definition of curiosity appropriate for your needs.

Individual Differences

Not everyone is equally curious. Curiosity can be viewed as both a stable personality feature (trait) and a condition that can be influenced (state). One researcher (Naylor) describes trait curiosity as individual differences in capacity to experience curiosity, and state curiosity as individual differences in response to a curiosity-arousing situation. Thus curiosity stimulation that sends one child into a zone of curiosity can send another into a zone of anxiety!

As the designer of a software product for children, what can you do to address individual differences in curiosity? Perhaps you could incorporate a diagnostic tool that allows you to assess the appropriate level of stimulation for the child user. Children whose score indicates a low tolerance for uncertainty could be routed to the software version that stimulates curiosity but reduces factors that could result in anxiety in low-curiosity children. These children, for example, might receive more guidance.

Stimulating curiosity through inquiry arousal plays an important role in gaining and sustaining learners' attention, the first component of the ARCS model.

Strategies That Promote Inquiry through Stimulating Curiosity

Fostering the scholarly attribute of curiosity in children is an important task for both media producers and educators. Providing children with adequate guidance while affording them the opportunities for exploration, however, is probably easier stated than accomplished. As mentioned earlier, not all children are highly curious and what might stimulate curiosity in some might result in anxiety for others, thus depressing attention all together. It becomes the job of the media producer and her team to recognize these differences and control the media elements to accommodate all learners. With this caveat in mind, here are some strategies for stimulating curiosity as an attention component, making note of whether each is more effective for gaining or sustaining attention, or both.

Strategy 1: A question as a hook (gaining attention). Use curiosity as a primary motivator to capture attention at the beginning of your media presentation by starting, for example, with a thought-provoking question. If this is a website, pose the question on the homepage.

Strategy 2: Conceptual conflict (gaining and sustaining attention). Introduce a conceptual conflict when possible. Children will feel compelled to explore the conflict until it is resolved. When the child has resolved the conceptual conflict, he will sense a feeling of satisfaction.

Strategy 3: An atmosphere for questions (sustaining attention). Create an atmosphere in which students feel comfortable about raising questions and can test their own hypotheses through discussion and brainstorming. Not only does this foster curiosity but it also helps build confidence. How can you do this when producing for a linear medium such as video? It's still possible especially when viewing will be done with a parent or a facilitator! For example, you could program in "reflection points" that encourage the child to ask questions. I have used this technique successfully on a number of projects. It encourages question-asking behavior and also helps reinforce the essential program content.

Strategy 4: Progressive disclosure (sustaining attention). This is appropriate for most media types, including video, multimedia, Web, and print. Show only one piece of the content or learning puzzle at a time using a new hook for each piece revealed such as What do you suppose . . . ? or What if . . . ? questions.

Strategy 5: Novelty (gaining attention). Incorporate elements that have a novel aspect. An odd-looking puppet, for example, may elicit a viewer's initial curiosity and attention, but to sustain that attention, you will have to incorporate relevance strategies as well.

Strategy 6: The right amount of stimulation (sustaining attention). In designing interactive media environments, be aware of the degree of stimulation that is being built into the learning situation. Remember, there are individual differences when it comes to curiosity. Some children will become anxious if the stimulus is too complex, too uncertain, or too novel. They may quickly leave the zone of curiosity and enter the zone of anxiety.

Strategy 7: Exploration (sustaining attention). Create media products that involve active exploration by the child. Learning by exploration (LBE) is one of the features of constructivism, a mode of facilitating learning by allowing children to construct their own meaning or conclusions. As producer/designer, you provide the children with the tools for exploration and they discover their own answers. Alternatively, you could create a problem-based learning environment (PBL) in which you provide the "problem" to be solved and the children must find a way of solving that problem. The first represents a bottom-up approach to exploration whereas the latter represents a top-down approach.

Strategy 8: Incongruity, contradiction, and mystery (sustaining attention). Children will want to explore the source of the incongruity, contradiction, or mystery in order to gather information that will satisfy their curiosity. For example, creating a graphic by combining a dinosaur with a pig and calling it a pigosaurus may have a five-year-old wondering what she missed in those dinosaur books! The effect would not be the same for a one- or two-year-old. With their limited experience, they would not even recognize the incongruity.

Strategy 9: Children as curiosity role models (sustaining attention). Whether you are producing software, a video, a television program, or creating a Web environment, incorporate children who will epitomize curiosity. They should be seen by viewers/users asking questions, engaging in specific exploration to resolve a question posed, and demonstrating enthusiasm. This strategy maintains attention because children enjoy watching other children. As you will learn in chapters 6–7, it can also be used to promote relevance and build confidence.

Stimulating curiosity is what inquiry arousal is all about. Yet from a motivational perspective, curiosity is more than just a strategy to acquire and sustain children's attention. To instill curiosity in children is to encourage their disposition to learn. To ignore its importance is to risk diminishing (if not losing) the endowment of curiosity conferred on all at birth.

VARIABILITY

The final ARCS category for the attention component is variability. CTW recognized the importance of variability for sustaining attention in selecting the magazine format for *Sesame Street*. Research shows that the preschool audience prefers a fast-paced format. The magazine format allowed the production staff a high degree of flexibility in creating short segments that maintained attention. Another benefit of this format was that segments that were not shown to be effective could be dropped and others added without impacting the overall program. The magazine format has also proven effective with older children and adults.

Strategies for Creating Variability

Strategy 1: Brief segments. Keep segments brief. This is true whether designing for Web, print, video, television, or a software product. CTW found that preschoolers' attention could rarely be maintained for more than three or four minutes in a single segment. Brevity also helps build expectations for success (you'll find out more about that in chapter 7).

Strategy 2: Opportunities for frequent response. Providing such opportunities is especially important when designing software applications. Children today expect a high degree of interactivity. Keller suggests intermingling information presentation screens with interactive screens and making those response requests require application of the content in a related task.

Strategy 3: Variation of visual elements. While it is important to maintain some design continuity (e.g., the general interface of a website), include visual variations within your design parameters to maintain attention. These could include, for example, appealing graphics, use of color, separation of content in boxes, and shapes.

Watch Out!

Young children are very easily distracted. While including variation in your presentation is good, try to avoid overdoing it, as attention may inadvertently be directed away from the central content. As children get older, they become better at selectively attending to the most important content.

Strategy 4: Formal features of the medium. Use the formal features of the medium for drawing attention to the salient aspects of the screen or page. Gerry Lesser calls this "screening out irrelevancies." Such irrelevancies can confuse the child and result in decreased attention. If you are producing a video or television program, for example, it is possible to zoom into the area of the frame where you want the child to focus. It is also possible to blur out irrelevant parts of the frame. Each medium has its own special features that can be used to narrow a child's focus. For example, the print medium can use white space around central content to draw attention to it.

Strategy 5: Pacing. When designing multimedia or software products, you can provide children with the option of varying the pacing. This helps address individual differences in learning styles and preferences, as well. For example, the more reflective learner will appreciate having more time to think about the content and self-regulate his learning. You will see that this strategy works not only for variability but also for building confidence (see chapter 7).

Strategy 6: Variety of elements. Vary the elements you use to present the content. Role play, games, scenarios, music, and animations are possible techniques.

Strategy 7: Voice inflections. Varying the vocal tone, inflection, and pacing can add interest to your media presentation and help draw attention to important content. Voice inflections are analogous to bolding, italics, and highlighting in the print media.

Strategy 8: Transitions and lead-ins. An effective method to add variety that is used in many electronic media presentations is creating lively transitions to bridge content. These transitions become expected and thus effectively signal the child to forthcoming changes. Because transitions are scattered throughout a presentation, they add variety and help sustain attention. Transitions can be animated or graphical, can include human or animal characters, and can be accompanied by music and/or sound effects. Shari Lewis, creator of *Lamb Chop's Play-Along* television program, sprinkled riddles throughout her program; children were tipped off to the upcoming segment by a lively visual and musical transition.

! Tips and Tactics

An Important Use of Transitions

Programs that incorporate commercial content should always include transitions to that content that clearly explains where the program ends and the commercial begins. Young children have difficulty distinguishing between fantasy and reality; not informing them of this distinction takes advantage of their vulnerability in this respect. Web-based projects that include advertising must likewise clearly mark their banner ads so that it is evident they present an advertising message.

Strategy 9: Special technical effects. Children find fast and slow motion segments appealing, as well as pixilation, which can be as attention riveting as animation. There are always new effects that can be easily accomplished in electronic mediums, but don't overuse technical effects.

Strategy 10: Production quality. Children are sophisticated when it comes to media and can readily distinguish the difference between high and low production quality. Maintain the highest production quality your budget can afford.

**Developmental Snapshot
The Child at Seven**

What a difference between six and seven! By comparison, the seven-year-old is more restrained, allowing her to actually listen to others instead of always knowing the answer (in her mind) or having to be top dog. She demonstrates more sensitivity toward the feelings of others. Reasoning abilities have dramatically increased as she takes in all that her world has to offer. She can now classify and sort out information in her head. In school, she wants to be successful and shows more persistence on learning tasks. Her personal space is important to her as she becomes her own person; her bedroom is her special place.

Note: Developmental snapshots are necessarily general and do not take into consideration wide variations in individual differences related to personality, learning, or physical development.

FINAL NOTE

Recalling expectancy-value theory discussed in chapters 1, 3, and 4, attention contributes to the value component. If you do not capture a child's attention and then sustain it for the duration of your message, you will not achieve your learning goals.

COMING UP NEXT . . .

The second motivational component that affects "value" is relevance. How we make our media products meaningful to children is the subject of Chapter 6.

PRODUCER'S CHECKLIST

❑ Attention is the first component of the ARCS model. It contributes to the "value" factor in expectancy-value theory.

- ❏ The three contributors to attention are
  - Perceptual arousal
  - Inquiry arousal
  - Variability
- ❏ Perceptual arousal can include any sensory stimulus that initially grabs a child's attention. Strategies include incongruity, surprise, novelty, and making the abstract concrete. The main purpose of perceptual arousal is to gain attention or regain lost attention.
- ❏ Inquiry arousal includes stimulating a child's curiosity and attitude of inquiry. Strategies include using a question as a hook, creating a conceptual conflict that the child will want to resolve, progressive disclosure, and encouraging active exploration through LBE- or PBL-structured learning environments. Inquiry arousal can be used to gain attention but is most effective for sustaining attention.
- ❏ Variability is used to sustain attention. Strategies include varying pace and providing a variety of visual and auditory elements.
- ❏ Consider individual differences in curiosity, learning styles, and other preferences when designing media for children.

DIGGING DEEPER

This chapter examined the concept of curiosity as a motivator for gaining and sustaining children's attention; you will find many references on curiosity in the following list.

Alberti, E. T., and Witryl, S. L. 1994. "The Relationship between Curiosity and Cognitive Ability in Third and Fifth Grade Children." *Journal of Genetic Psychology* 155, no. 2: 129–45.

Arnone, M., and Grabowski, B. 1992. "Effects on Children's Achievement and Curiosity of Variations in Learner Control over an Interactive Video Lesson." *Educational Technology Research and Development* 40, no. 1: 15–28.

Arnone, M., Grabowski, B., and Rynd, C. 1994. "Curiosity as a Personality Variable Influencing Learning in a Learner-Controlled Lesson with and without Advisement." *Educational Technology Research and Development* 42, no. 1: 5–20.

Arnone, M. P., and Small, Ruth V. 1995. "Arousing and Sustaining Curiosity: Lessons from the ARCS Model." In *17th Annual Proceedings of Selected Research and Development Presentations, National Convention of the Association for Educational Communications and Technology* (Anaheim, Calif.), 1–15.

Berlyne, D. E. 1960. *Conflict, Arousal, and Curiosity.* New York: McGraw-Hill.

Beswick, D. 1968. "Cognitive Process Theory of Individual Differences in Curiosity." In H. Day, D. Berlyne, and D. Hunt, eds., *Intrinsic Motivation: A New Direction in Learning.* Toronto: Rinehart & Winston of Canada.

Day, H. I. 1982. "Curiosity and the Interested Explorer." *NSPI Journal,* May, 19–22.

Gorlitz, D. 1987. *Curiosity, Imagination, and Play: On the Development of Spontaneous Cognitive and Motivational Processes.* Hillsdale, N.J.: Erlbaum.

Keller, J. M. 1987. "The Systematic Process of Motivational Design." *Performance and Instruction,* 1–8.

Loewenstein, G. 1994. "The Psychology of Curiosity: A Review and Reinterpretation." *Psychological Bulletin* 116, no. 1: 75–98.

Malone, T. W. 1981. "Toward a Theory of Intrinsically Motivating Instruction." *Cognitive Science* 4: 335–69.

Maw, W., and Maw, E. 1964. *An Exploratory Study into the Measurement of Curiosity in Elementary School Children.* Cooperative Research Project no. 801.

Naylor, F. D. 1981. "A State-Trait Curiosity Inventory." *Australian Psychologist* 16, no. 2: 172–83.

Rice, M., Huston, A., and Wright, J. 1983. "The Forms of Television: Effects on Children's Attention, Comprehension, and Social Behavior." In M. Meyer, ed., *Children and the Formal Features of Television: Approaches and Findings of Experimental and Formative Research.* New York: Saur.

Small, R. V., and Arnone, M. P. 2000. *Turning Kids On to Research: The Power of Motivation.* Englewood, Colo.: Libraries Unlimited.

6

ESTABLISHING RELEVANCE

Relevance is the second component required to establish the value of your media project. How does your project meet the perceived needs of the children you are addressing? How meaningful is your content to them? Have you tied it in some way to their personal experiences? All these questions are important as you design strategies that will address this critical motivational component. In this chapter, we will explore relevance in detail and review some of the motivational theories and principles that influence relevance. I will suggest numerous strategies you can incorporate into your media product that will help accomplish the goal of establishing relevance.

THE RELEVANCE COMPONENT OF THE ARCS MODEL

The ARCS model includes three primary categories of strategies for establishing relevance:

- Goal orientation
- Motive matching
- Familiarity

We will look at each of these individually and apply them to children's media.

Have you been thinking that motivation is so important that you will throw in everything you have to a media presentation to make sure all bases are covered? Lots of people think that way, but remember that too much of anything good can be a bad thing. Check out the following feature section.

❗ Tips and Tactics

Is It Possible to Have Too Many Strategies?

It certainly is! While you might think that adding a multitude of motivational strategies to your media project will guarantee a highly motivated audience, it doesn't work that way. If children find the learning task is already highly relevant to them, or if they are already very motivated, they will find a glut of motivational strategies to be distracting or annoying. That is why your audience motivational analysis is important. It helps you determine what types of strategies and how many are necessary.

GOAL ORIENTATION

Your media product must provide your viewers with knowledge or skills that they can apply to accomplishing meaningful goals. Young children will not be thinking in precise terms such as "goals," so you must create relevance by providing reasons for viewing or participating in your media product. It could be a short-term goal or reason, or it could be a future aspiration. For example, young children contemplate what they might become when they grow up; how can your media product tap into that wondering? With older children who are capable of articulating their goals, you can directly relate your product with the achievement of a school-related objective or other practical goal. Let's consider some strategies that address goal orientation either directly or indirectly.

The Research Says...

Engaging in authentic tasks and problems is more meaningful to students. Such tasks can mirror the scientific process of discovery or provide real-life applications of the content. Authentic tasks increase students' intrinsic motivation to learn because of their perceived utility (Pintrich and Schunk 2002).

Strategies for Connecting with Goal Orientation

Strategy 1: Clarity and relevance of objectives. Be clear about the objectives of your media presentation. This does not mean that you have to state them in a tedious or lackluster fashion such as, "When you finish viewing this video, you will be able to identify the factors that influence the weather." On the contrary, to address this from a motivational perspective, you will want to make students excited about what they will learn, such as, "Imagine being able to forecast the weather so that you can plan a picnic or a visit to the zoo! You can do that if you know the right clues to look for! In this video, you will discover. . . ." Be clear but present your objectives in an exciting manner that piques their interest and lets them know that the learning objectives will be useful to them.

Strategy 2: Children as presenters of defined objectives. Have children present your objectives for you! Since your audience will identify with children their own age or a bit older, you will automatically increase relevance. As in strategy 1, the objectives should be clear with readily apparent usefulness.

Strategy 3: Connecting with intrinsic motivation. Relate to the intrinsic value of learning. The topic is presented as fun to learn or as an interesting topic to know about.

Strategy 4: Individual differences and interests. Use the results of your front-end assessment to determine age-related and gender-related interests, and make sure you address these when presenting the goals of your media project.

Strategy 5: Process of goal attainment. Make the process of attaining the goals exciting and meaningful. Active learning (the child is an active participant in his learning as opposed to a passive receiver of information) and problem-based learning (the child is a problem solver in a realistic scenario confronting a problem that may have more than one correct solution) are two approaches that increase relevance. Web and software developers are in a great position to utilize these approaches. (See "Digging Deeper" at the end of this chapter for suggestions on resources to learn more about these approaches.)

While all these strategies are useful in goal orientation, strategy 5, process of goal attainment, is especially important. Simply presenting information with some bells and whistles to beef up a media presentation can still be boring and uninteresting to a child audience. An excellent example of using a problem-based learning approach is the NASA-funded project entitled Kids as Airborne Mission Scientists (KaAMS) directed by Barbara Grabowski and Tiffany Koszalka. The project offers a wonderful Web-based resource for educators and includes lesson plans and numerous resources they can use with their young scientists, including graphics, videos, animations, charts, and links to other resources. The KaAMS project embraces a problem-based learning approach to attaining instructional goals in which children are given a problem scenario or question about an event, such as the eruption of a volcano, and the kids (as Airborne Mission Scientists) solve the problem or answer the question. They must use a scientific approach for investigating the problem, propose ideas and search for information to support their ideas, collect and analyze their data, and finally propose and communicate their solutions.

MOTIVE MATCHING

Motive matching considers "how" you present your message. It embodies learning styles, preferences, values, and other needs, real or perceived. You can create a more appealing media product by incorporating strategies that address the potential needs of your audience. Recall from chapter 3 the importance of your audience motivational analysis. When you begin to design strategies for motive matching, you need to refer to that analysis. What did you discover about your audience that can help you identify potential motives that increase the relevance of your offering? There are a number of strategies you can build into your media product to address this aspect of relevance.

Take 2

Motives and Needs

While goal orientation, the first category of strategies for creating relevance, clearly is grounded in the *content* we must present to learners, without addressing children's possible motives as they relate to their real or perceived needs, learning may not occur. For example, Maslow's hierarchy of human needs holds that physiological and safety needs must be met before higher needs can be addressed, such as esteem needs (mastering learning tasks, etc.). How can we expect to create relevance for learning if our audience is hungry?

Theoretically Speaking...

In chapter 3, you were introduced to David McClelland's achievement motivation theory. His research provided empirical support for three basic human motives:

- Need for achievement
- Need for affiliation
- Need for power

According to this theory, individuals may be higher or lower in one or more of these motives. For example, children with a high need for affiliation love opportunities to work cooperatively with other children, especially if competition is kept to a minimum. These children enjoy the social aspects of learning. Within this group, some children may also have a need for power, but perhaps it is not as strong as their need for affiliation. All of us have all three needs, but one is usually stronger than the others.

Consider what strategies you could design into your media project to address these needs.

Strategies for Motive Matching

Strategy 1: Need for achievement. Children who have a high need for achievement enjoy a moderate level of challenge in which they have the potential for success. They are interested in achieving their personal best and often like working independently. These children will appreciate your testing their competence. In designing a Web-based learning environment or software application, include challenge opportunities such as games or miniquizzes that test their knowledge or comprehension of the topic or principle you are presenting. Include note-taking functions and a way to track personal progress. The design of print-based materials could easily include this strategy. Video and television programs could offer support materials, either Web-based or print-based to incorporate the strategy. Make sure the video or televised program lets them know they can "take the challenge" after viewing to create positive anticipation.

Strategy 2: Need for affiliation/tools for collaboration. Create an environment within your media design that affords children who are high in need for affiliation with tools for collaboration and building community, opportunities for communicating and interacting with other children. Web-based projects can accomplish this strategy on all levels—locally, regionally, nationally, and even internationally. Children high in need for affiliation will love cooperative opportunities to explore solutions and collaborate with others.

!Tips and Tactics

A Web-Based Collaborative Project

One Web-based media project for children enhances creativity through storytelling. The strategy employed appeals to children high in need for affiliation. The developers created a storytelling system in which children from all around the world work collaboratively to create a story. Each child contributes one sentence until the story is complete, carefully building on the work of each other so that the story flows naturally.

Strategy 3: Need for power. Provide leadership opportunities. For example, if you are producing a software product, consider creating games, simulations, or role-playing scenarios in which the child can assume a leadership role. Opportunities for friendly competition also address this need.

Strategy 4: Feedback. Provide a means of feedback whenever possible. For example, in Web-based and software products, this is accomplished with specific response feedback on incorrect answers.

Strategy 5: Modeling. Incorporate positive role models in your video, television, or multimedia product. A role model could be someone with whom children in your target audience can identify. Role models can include adults with expertise in the area of their interest, other children who have accomplished goals of interest to the audience, sports figures, and other celebrities. Modeling is a strategy that increases value and adds to the likelihood that the desired behavior will be adopted. An alternative to a live model for print-based media is a quote or story about a significant individual the child knows from viewing media.

Strategy 6: Enthusiasm. Select dynamic spokespersons (both adults or children) for your media project who can demonstrate genuine enthusiasm for the topic on-camera and/or through voice-overs. If you are not planning to use a spokesperson, you can also generate enthusiasm through the use of vibrant text, quotes, and testimonials.

These strategies, taken cumulatively, signal a call for developing media products for the child audience that are adaptive to their needs, abilities, and learning styles. Aim for flexibility in your design, especially with interactive learning technologies that afford such opportunities. Encourage self-expression and exploration in an environment that accommodates their learning preferences.

FAMILIARITY

Another way to increase relevance is to incorporate strategies that connect with what you know to be typical of children's experiences in the age-group you are targeting. At a basic level, this means presenting your content using language and concepts that the child can understand. Understanding the developmental level of your target audience is critical to knowing how to effectively introduce new information. As you will see from the suggested strategies, familiarity also includes personalizing the learning experience.

Strategies for Generating Familiarity

Strategy 1: Building on the familiar. Start with the familiar and introduce new concepts to your audience that build on what it already knows. For example, I was designing a website for children to teach them evaluation skills for the World Wide Web. One educator I was working with suggested that we start with the child's familiar world of books, explore how they could tell a good book from a poor one, and work from there to websites. There was some overlap, and her strategy worked well.

Strategy 2: Developmentally appropriate language. Use language that can be easily understood by members of the target audience. Using words above their level will result in a quick turnoff, and regaining their attention may be difficult.

Strategy 3: Personalizing the learning. Personalize the learning by providing examples from the experience of the spokesperson in your video that relate to the learning. A child spokesperson could relate how she uses what she learned in real life. For example, if your video is teaching children to use 911, you could personalize it by having your child spokesperson tell how she had to call 911 because her grandfather collapsed at home and she was the only one around.

Strategy 4: Preexisting interests. Tap into the research you conducted during your front-end analysis that informed you of the specific interests and preferences of children in your target audience. What programs do they watch? Who are their favorite celebrities? What are the social interests of children in your specific target age range? Answers to these questions will help you present the content in a way that appeals to their preexisting interests.

Strategy 5: Concrete examples. Provide concrete examples that are grounded in what is already familiar to the audience. For example, you can sometimes make connections by using analogies or metaphors to present new concepts.

Strategy 6: Audience-generated examples. Ask your audience for examples of how members could use the content being presented in your media product in their own lives. This could easily be accomplished with older children in a Web-based project that incorporates a forum for sharing experiences with other visitors to the website. In a video presentation, you could accomplish this by programming video stop-downs or what I

ESTABLISHING RELEVANCE 71

earlier referred to as reflection points, where the tape, CD, or DVD is paused, and children can share their own examples. Print-based media can include a special place where children old enough to write could record their experiences.

Strategy 7: Choices. Whenever possible, provide choices for your audience members that allow them to pursue specific interests within a broad topic or select a mode of presentation that fits their learning style or preference. In a Web-based environment, for example, you could give learners who prefer an audio mode the option of listening to a narrative of the text as they read along.

Watch Out!

Just as good teachers can inspire motivation and ineffective teachers can be demotivating, the media products we develop for the child audience can positively or negatively affect a child's motivation to learn. The systematic analysis and design of the motivational objectives and strategies for your product will help avoid potential negative motivational outcomes.

Pop quiz: Why is it important, as media producers, to have a general understanding of motivational principles? Take the eight-year-old, for example. Understanding curiosity as a motivational variable helps you to understand him. Read the following developmental snapshot feature section.

Developmental Snapshot
The Child at Eight

The eight-year-old epitomizes the construct of curiosity defined in chapter 5. He is constantly exploring his environment and manipulating the objects of that environment in an effort to truly understand them. He is an active explorer in all respects, and this includes his curiosity about himself as well as those around him. You will often hear the eight-year-old testing his ideas on the adults and children in his life. He loves interacting with adults, as well as just listening in; he is a sponge absorbing everything they say and attempting to make sense of it. Friends are important, most often same-sex friends at this age. School is something he looks forward to especially because it is a social place where he connects with his friends. What strategies for increasing relevance does this developmental snapshot suggest to you?

Note: Developmental snapshots are necessarily general and do not take into consideration wide variations in individual differences related to personality, learning, or physical development.

FINAL NOTE

Now you have learned the two components of the ARCS model that address the value factor of expectancy-value theory—attention and relevance (see figure 4). You have also discovered some practical strategies for addressing these components with a child audience in a media-related project.

COMING UP NEXT ...

While value is a crucial and necessary component for learning, it is insufficient to guarantee success. Equally important is promoting the expectation that the child can be successful, if he attempts to learn or perform according to the educational objectives you have defined. How we design a learning environment for our media products that fosters a positive expectation for success is the subject of chapter 7, "Building Confidence."

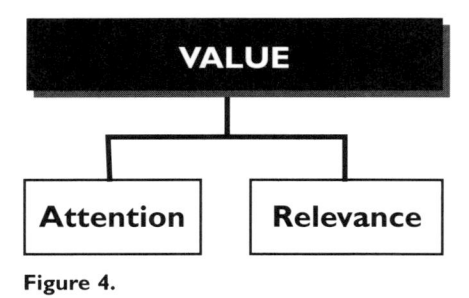

Figure 4.

PRODUCER'S CHECKLIST

❏ Relevance is the second component of the ARCS model. Like attention, relevance contributes to the "value" factor in expectancy-value theory.
❏ The three categories of relevance are:
   • Goal orientation
   • Motive matching
   • Familiarity
❏ Goal orientation increases relevance by identifying the utility of your media message in the child's life. Strategies include clearly presenting learning objectives in a way that targets the interests of the child audience. You must ask the question, how can I make learning this content appealing to children? Another strategy is using children to help present goals and having them relate the utility of learning as it applies to their lives.
❏ Motive matching relates more to the "how" of presenting your message than to the actual content by addressing the needs and values of your audience. Strategies include providing opportunities to fulfill a need for achievement, need for affiliation, and need for power, as well as modeling. It is important to relate back to your front-end analysis when you plan your motive matching strategies.
❏ Familiarity is an important relevance category and involves assessing the developmental level of your audience. Strategies include using age-appropriate language, building from the familiar to the unfamiliar in presenting content, and using concrete examples.
❏ In order to expect learning to occur, children's basic physiological and safety needs must be met.

DIGGING DEEPER

For most references on Keller's ARCS model, see chapters 3–4. You may also be interested in the following additional references.

Brophy, Jere. 1998. *Motivating Students to Learn.* Boston: McGraw-Hill.
Keller, John. 1999. "Motivation in Cyber Learning Environments." *International Journal of Educational Technology* 1, no. 1: 7–30.
Maslow, Abraham. 1962. *Toward a Psychology of Being.* Princeton, N.J.: Van Nostrand.
McClelland, David. 1961. *The Achieving Society.* Princeton, N.J.: Van Nostrand.
Pintrich, Paul R., and Schunk, Dale H. 2002. *Motivation in Education: Theory, Research, and Applications.* 2d ed. Upper Saddle River, N.J.: Merrill Prentice-Hall.

7

BUILDING AND REINFORCING CONFIDENCE

Confidence is the third component of Keller's ARCS model, and it relates to the second factor of expectancy-value theory: expectancy for success. You must ensure that children not only value the message you are bringing them but also can successfully accomplish the task. Sometimes this means challenging a preexisting belief or attribution; it almost always requires incorporating strategies designed to give your audience a successful experience. Confidence is crucial to the developing child's self-esteem and a sense of his emerging mastery of the world around him. In this chapter, we will explore motivational principles that affect a child's confidence, review the main categories for addressing confidence as proposed in Keller's ARCS model, and consider numerous strategies you can incorporate into your media product that will help accomplish the goal of building and reinforcing confidence.

MOTIVATIONAL CONSTRUCTS RELATED TO CONFIDENCE

Several motivational constructs and principles should be noted before we proceed to the confidence component of ARCS and related strategies. These principles help elucidate the rationale for the subsequent suggested strategies and share some commonalities.

Self-efficacy

Self-efficacy is an important construct that relates to a child's confidence in his abilities and expectation for success. It is the major component of Albert Bandura's social cognitive theory. Self-efficacy relates to a child's perceptions of his capability to produce a particular behavior or accomplish a task. Notice the word "perceptions." It is the child's judgment of what he can do, not what he may be capable of accomplishing. This is an important distinction, as perceptions will determine the actions a child takes. A series of prior failures, for example, could lead to beliefs about abilities that in turn lower the child's self-efficacy and result in what Jere Brophy calls "failure syndrome." Or the child may have experienced the physiological symptoms of anxiety before engaging in a task, leading him to believe that he must not have the ability to succeed at that task. The child may generalize this perceived inability to other similar tasks. There could be a number of contributing factors. Parents and teachers can be sensitive to the behaviors of children in their charge, looking for cues as to their self-beliefs of efficacy.

As media producers, you are unlikely to have such contact on a regular basis with your audience. Your product must also appeal to a wide audience with a range of self-beliefs, some high, some low. Yet, by understanding the importance of self-efficacy, you can incorporate motivational strategies in your media product that will address this important motivational concern. Providing opportunities for success, immediate feedback when possible (easier for multimedia applications), chunking learning content, and linking effort with outcomes are several of the strategies you can employ and that will be discussed later in this chapter. An increase in self-efficacy can result in longer persistence on tasks, more successes, and a better self-monitoring of what needs to be accomplished for success on a particular task.

Self-fulfilling Prophecy

Another closely related construct is self-fulfilling prophecy, briefly mentioned in chapter 3. It is based on the notion that individuals behave according to what others consistently expect of them. Sometimes those expectations are based on secondhand information, appearance, ethnicity, socioeconomic level, body build, or simply a first impression. Often they are erroneous. Unconsciously, in many cases, expectations are conveyed through interactions with the child by significant others. Unfortunately, if the expectations are negative, the child may eventually behave as expected, and the cycle of self-fulfilling prophecy (SFP) begins. Combine a low ex-

BUILDING AND REINFORCING CONFIDENCE 77

pectation for success with fear of failure, and you have a child who puts little effort into achieving learning goals.

On the other hand, in the movie *My Fair Lady* the opposite happens. Professor Higgins had high expectations of a poor, uneducated flower girl named Eliza Doolittle, and under his tutelage she blossomed into a charming woman with apparent class and grace. His consistent expectations resulted in a positive transformation. As media producers, you can help shape children's positive expectations for success by acknowledging the potential of your audience as a whole and providing tools for success. Many of the strategies for addressing self-efficacy are also applicable for SFP.

One final note on SFP. After completing her background research on SFP for a recent class I was coteaching, one of my graduate students (a teacher) was impressed by her school principal's hard-and-fast rule, which now made sense to her. His rule was that there was to be no casual commenting in the teachers' lounge, good or bad, about any student. Since it would be difficult to confine comments to only positive remarks in casual conversation, this was a good rule. I commend this principal's integrity and the strength of his beliefs about teacher expectations and the power of SFP!

ATTRIBUTION THEORY

Think about the following question as it pertains to you; really take a moment and consider it: How do you explain your successes and failures?

I am guessing that you probably attribute most of your successes to internal factors. Okay, it is just a guess, but one of the clues is your interest in reading a book like this that deals with motivational issues. Now, back to attribution theory. A number of motivational constructs can be subsumed under the umbrella of attribution theory proposed by Bernard Weiner. According to this theory, there are four explanations that someone will give for successes and failures. Two are internal explanations and two are external. Let me provide a hypothetical example as a means of explaining. An educational video on a science concept has been shown to several children who are given a comprehension test on the video's content after viewing. A child with an internal attribution who did well on the test would attribute her success to ability and/or effort.

- Ability ("I did really well on the test because I am good at science!")
- Effort ("I did well on the test because I really listened and watched the video!")

How might a child with an internal attribution explain a poor result on the video test? It might sound something like this:

- Ability ("I'm not good at science. That's why I didn't do well on the test.")
- Effort ("I wasn't paying attention to the video, so I did poorly on the test.")

How about a child who attributes success and failure to external factors, specifically task difficulty and luck? These might be the possible explanations, starting with the external attributions for success.

- Task difficulty ("That was such an easy test; that's why I did well.")
- Luck ("Wow! I guess it helped that I wore my lucky shirt today!")

Here's what failure might sound like for the external attributions:

- Task difficulty ("That video was hard to follow, and the test was way too hard! That's why I did so poorly.")
- Luck ("I should have worn my lucky shirt today!")

These attributions are related to what Julian Rotter and other researchers call locus of control. A child who feels she has little control over a situation, including her learning, has a perceived external locus of control and will likely attribute either positive or negative outcomes to external conditions. An internal locus of control would be characterized by internal attributions such as ability and effort. While ability is perceived as being stable, luck would be considered unstable. Attribution retraining, suggested by Jere Brophy, can help children who are discouraged about their ability to learn. Brophy suggests strategies that help learners focus on the present task rather than on past failures and attribute failure to a lack of effort or other reason that can be addressed and changed. For example, a discouraged child should be encouraged to perceive her problem as not related to ability (stable and uncontrollable) but to inadequate strategies for learning the content (changeable and controllable). Alternative approaches to the learning task(s) can also help such children.

Most of the time, we do want children to attribute their successes and failures to internal factors. I say "most of the time" because there are times when an internal attribution is not appropriate, such as when a child says something like "I am just too stupid to learn this!" This attitude, or possibly even sincere belief, definitely needs attribution retraining focusing on effort as opposed to ability. Such a statement could be expected from a child with learning disabilities. Research suggests that children with learning disabilities are more likely to attribute successes to external factors and failures to internal factors. There are also times when an external attribution may actually be appropriate and correct. For example, what if the test in the video example I gave earlier really was at a difficulty level that was either too high or too low for the children taking the test?

One last motivation principle related to attribution theory is worth mentioning here. Repeated experiences of failure, the perception that the child has no control over her outcomes (external locus of control), and not realizing that her own actions have a bearing on her lack of success contribute to a condition known as learned helplessness, briefly referred to in chapter 3. Research suggests that learned helplessness is sometimes the result of many cumulative early failures. These children, who often come to believe in their own lack of ability, must be helped to view their ability as capable of being improved through practice. They will require more process-oriented as opposed to product-oriented learning experiences and the opportunities to experience frequent, albeit small, successes. Breaking the learning into smaller chunks with specific feedback on each chunk is useful for achieving frequent successes.

FLOW

Have you ever been so involved in an activity that you lost track of time? Perhaps it was a sports-related activity, a new software application you were learning, or a research topic you were exploring. Whatever activity it was, chances are you were in a state of "flow."

What's Flow?

Mihaly Csikszentmihalyi (1988) originated flow theory several decades ago as a doctoral student in Human Development at the University of Chicago. His research involved interviews with 175 people who were driven by intrinsic motivation. "Flow" is an experience characterized by "intense involvement, deep concentration, clarity of goals, and feedback, loss of sense of time, lack of self-consciousness leading to autotelic, that is, intrinsically rewarding experience."

If you have experienced flow, you know how it feels. I want you to think back on the last time you experienced flow as described in the previous Take 2 feature section. What were you doing? Place a check mark next to each box below that accurately reflects your situation during that space of time.

- ❏ Your goals were clear.
- ❏ You felt challenged but not overwhelmed; you had enough of the necessary skills for what you were doing.
- ❏ There were no distractions.
- ❏ You became intensely involved, losing track of time.
- ❏ Your actions and your awareness were fused.
- ❏ Your actions were fueled by an intrinsic motivation (autotelic); you wanted to do this—you didn't have to do it.
- ❏ Self-consciousness disappeared; you hardly even noticed your physical surroundings.
- ❏ Whatever you were doing, you were receiving some kind of feedback that you were "on track."
- ❏ You were not concerned about failure.
- ❏ While you were engaged in this activity, you forgot about your other problems; they were irrelevant to what you were doing at the time.

If the previous statements capture your experience, you were definitely in a flow state. You were probably extremely productive too. Although experiencing flow is wonderful, no one can remain in a flow state of mind indefinitely. Being there is partially dependent on the environment as well as the individual.

As media producers, how do you create an environment that is conducive to flow? For now, I will limit myself to interactive learning environments. Watching television and videos is just not as conducive to a flow state because little effort is required. Deliberate effort, a mental and/or physical "stretch," is essential for flow. To engender this type of effort and experience, producers of interactive media products can use the technologies at their disposal, combined with a good instructional/motivational plan, to create learning environments that tap into the inherent interests of the child audience and stimulate curiosity. Electronic learning environments must also offer them some sense of control or freedom over the activities in the

BUILDING AND REINFORCING CONFIDENCE

environment (even though there should be an overall structure) and should ensure that help is easily accessible. It should also offer a mechanism for providing feedback on progress. Knowing that help and feedback are easily accessible will encourage children to linger in their zones of curiosity long enough to fall into a true state of flow. Such media products will promote learning that is self-motivating and self-reinforcing.

The Confidence Component of the ARCS Model

The ARCS model includes three primary categories of strategies for building confidence. They are:

- Learning requirements
- Success opportunities
- Personal responsibility

Each category will be explained and applied to children's media with a number of examples and strategies.

LEARNING REQUIREMENTS

Children's expectancy for success increases if they have a clear picture of what is expected of them. How you present the learning requirements, regardless of the presentation media you are bringing into play, is also important. Considerations include sensitivity, flexibility, and a supportive environment. You might also want to consider presenting learning goals as opposed to performance goals, as research suggests they may be more effective (see the following).

The Research Says...

Learning goals are more effective than performance goals for helping children accomplish learning tasks. Performance goals require a high level of confidence because they are perceived to be connected with ability, whereas learning goals focus on the effort as a means of achieving goals (which in turn contribute to an increase in ability). Children who are fearful of exposing their perceived lack of ability to meet a performance criterion will tend to avoid challenges or perform poorly. Focusing on learning goals helps children overcome obstacles and thus activates their ability (Dweck 1986).

Strategies for Addressing Learning Requirements

Let's consider some strategies that will address this first category for building confidence, learning requirements.

Strategy 1: Clear expectations. Provide clear expectations for what you expect the child to be able to do as a result of watching your video or television program, interacting with your Web-based project or software application, or reading your print-based materials. What should they know, how much work is involved, how will they be evaluated, how much will they be allowed to participate in goal setting, and how will they know if they are progressing according to your plan are all questions the school-age child should have answered. If the learning requirements are very clear, learners will have a higher expectation for success. Too often learners experience undue anxiety because expectations are vague and poorly defined.

Strategy 2: Adaptability/flexibility. Be prepared, if necessary, to modify learning goals to be compatible with student abilities, learning styles, and values. Producers of computer-based and Web applications are in the best position to utilize adaptive strategies to support and accommodate variations in learners. By collecting initial and in-use data from the child user (possibly a questionnaire built into the front end of the system, as well as tracking learner input throughout the learning process), the system can revise expectations, change instructional modalities to suit the learning style of the user, and accommodate the curriculum based on ability level. Beyond that, there is even evidence now that a computer-based system can be designed to support the dynamic changes in motivation that can occur during the course of a learning episode. See the following Research Says feature box.

The Research Says...

John Keller supports the design of multimedia and computer-based software that senses a learner's motivation and can respond adaptively. In a study that explored the effects of a prototype designed to respond to changes in a learner's motivation during computer-based instruction, Song and Keller found the ARCS model to be instrumental and effective for designing the motivational support for the adaptive system (Song and Keller 2001).

Strategy 3: Concrete examples. Use concrete examples of what achieving learning goals looks like. For example, a video could show other kids' accomplishments, a website could have a special section that displays examples from other children who have completed the assigned task(s) or "mission" (if you choose to use more exciting terms).

Strategy 4: Learning environment. Create a safe, nurturing learning environment as the setting for addressing learning requirements. This will help lower the anxiety of students with low self-efficacy. A familiar environment is also effective. My company produced an instructional video teaching children how to use 911 in an emergency. The setting was a studio rendition of a children's makeshift TV studio set up in the family garage; child actors played the parts of on-camera hosts and TV crew. The familiarity of the setting was appealing to viewers.

Strategy 5: Anxiety avoidance/spokesperson qualities. Generate trust by selecting a spokesperson or character for your presentation who exudes sensitivity and a nurturing personality. If you do not plan to use on-camera talent, you can accomplish this with voice-overs if you choose someone whose voice conveys the same qualities.

Strategy 5: Process emphasis. Excite students about the process of learning, not just what is expected as outcomes. Emphasizing process is especially helpful to children with learned helplessness or self-beliefs of low ability. Problem-based learning approaches, discussed in chapter 6, emphasize process.

Strategy 6: Theme approach. When possible, design your media product to be integrated into a holistic learning package, collaborating with other subjects and experts, and assimilating your media product into a broader theme.

Strategy 7: Personal relevancy. Make the learning requirements personally relevant to your audience. If you think this belongs in the previous chapter (relevance strategies), you are correct. But it is also important when presenting the learning requirements and thus affects confidence as well. Creative scriptwriters and instructional designers can frame learning requirements in a way that "hooks" the audience using personal relevancy. To do this, you have to know your audience and their interests. No problem. You did your homework well during the front-end analysis!

SUCCESS OPPORTUNITIES

Strategies for Creating Success Opportunities

Keller cautions that after creating an expectancy for success, it is important that learners have a chance to succeed at the tasks they undertake. There are many strategies you could use for creating success opportunities. You will find more than a dozen strategies below, each one grounded in one or more of the motivational constructs and principles discussed earlier in this chapter. You should be able to think of many more once you focus on the specific medium in which you will be working and on your learning content.

Strategy 1: Tools of the trade. Provide your audience with a set of tools or strategies that will help them learn the content you are presenting. For example, a software or Web-based product could include a note-taking function with a learning aid or brief tutorial on how to best utilize note taking. Regardless of the medium in which you are planning your project, you could include study plans, self-tests, monitoring aids, helpful conventions (like the ones used in this book, but for kids), and other tools to facilitate success. (More on this later in the chapter when we discuss message design.)

Strategy 2: Make it fun! Think entertainment. Think marketing. Remember, you have to sell a child on learning. Make your media product fun to watch, interact with, or read. It will definitely result in greater effort, which equates to increased opportunities for success. If you are looking for some neat design ideas, read *Designing for Children: Marketing Design That Speaks to Kids,* by Catherine Fishel. It provides great images and insights into marketing designs that kids like. I like Catherine's simple, direct philosophy for a successful design for a child—it delights, informs, and satisfies.

Strategy 3: Practice, practice, practice. Provide opportunities to practice new skills or apply new knowledge in a meaningful way during the media experience or as soon as possible after it. Give them hands-on experience as much as possible!

Strategy 4: Chunking. Break the content into bite-size chunks. For example, videos can be produced with short modules followed by practice opportunities or reviews. Chunking content with follow-up soon after gives learners more opportunities to succeed, which is especially important for those with lower ability levels or motivational problems.

Strategy 5: Informative feedback. In a Web or interactive environment, feedback should be corrective and let the child know why the response was wrong, possibly branching to an alternative representation of the same content for children with different learning styles. The feedback should be immediate or as close to the time of the performance as possible.

Strategy 6: Remediation opportunities. This strategy complements strategy 5 in that children whose responses were incorrect could be branched to a remedial segment based on the particular incorrect response given and the misconception it represents.

Strategy 7: Guidance and help mechanisms. Children can be offered a recommended procedure (advisement) for learning, even if they chose to follow another route to achieve the outcomes. Help mechanisms in Web and software products should always be available and easily accessible.

Strategy 8: Anticipating potential obstacles. Anticipate potential obstacles to learning and eliminate as many as you can. Some of these obstacles could include learned helplessness, fear of failure, or physical disabilities. While your media product must first appeal to the general population of your target audience, you should also try to implement measures to help such children.

Strategy 9: Mastery learning. Incorporate measurements for success based on mastery of concepts as opposed to competition only or ranking performance against other learners.

Strategy 10: Support materials. Design a range of support materials for students with different reading abilities, special needs, or disabilities. Plan carefully and be prepared to meet needs promptly so that valuable time and enthusiasm are not lost. Television programs often have nonbroadcast support materials available in print form or on the Web. Videos could include print support materials as well, or post them on the Web.

Strategy 11: The right level of challenge. Children should find learning to be challenging, relevant, and doable. Factors affecting the challenge level include age and ability levels. If there is little or no challenge, the child will be bored and withdraw mentally from the learning process. It if is too difficult, the child will withdraw due to anxiety. Whether you are producing for a linear or an interactive medium, an easy-to-difficult sequence is usually effective and conducive to flow.

Strategy 12: Time and pacing. Learners should be able to vary pacing in interactive learning environments to adapt to their competency levels. Slow students will be less anxious about learning if they can spend more time on task. Control over time and pacing encourages persistence on task, and persistence is related to better achievement. Some children may fall into a state of flow if time constraints are removed and they can freely explore a topic.

Strategy 13: Freedom! But with some order. . . . Freedom triggers flow. (This strategy complements strategy 11.) Activities in which learners can make their own decisions, learn new skills, and work at their own pace will bolster confidence dramatically while increasing intrinsic motivation. With young learners, this can and probably should happen in an ordered atmosphere, as Csikszentmihalyi suggests. Children need rules to provide clarity and reduce the potential for anxiety.

PERSONAL RESPONSIBILITY

How can you convey to the children in your audience that they are responsible for their own learning and accomplishments? Here are a number of strategies that you can consider; some are more appropriate for interactive mediums and others can be used in video, television, and print. Attributional feedback is an important one (see the Theoretically Speaking feature box below).

Theoretically Speaking...

Keller (1987) stresses the importance of providing students with attributional feedback that emphasizes effort and ability with specific attention to the causes of success:

- You're really trying hard (effort).
- See, you did it on your own (ability).
- I liked the way you solved that problem (ability).

Strategies for Fostering Personal Responsibility

You may notice a slight overlap between some of the following strategies and those already suggested in this book. That is because some strategies can apply to more than one component or category within a component. A particular relevance strategy, for example, might have the effect of both increasing relevance and building confidence.

Strategy 1: Effort. Equate effort with success. And stress the quality of effort as opposed to simply the amount of effort.

Strategy 2: Self-regulation and appraisal. Provide the child with a means of regulating and appraising her learning throughout the process. It could be as simple as a paper-based checklist for linear media products or a periodic pop-up window that checks for understanding in a computer-based environment. The more control the child has over her learning, the more invested in it she will be.

Strategy 3: Frequent opportunities for success. This strategy complements strategy 4 under "Success Opportunities": chunking. While children do better with brief segments or modules because of the reduced cognitive load they afford (chunking), they also develop more confidence and are willing take on more responsibility for their learning when they begin experiencing success more often.

Strategy 4: Attribution retraining. Jere Brophy advocates attribution retraining for learners who have a tendency to attribute their successes and failures to lack of ability. Attribution retraining was introduced earlier in this chapter under "Attribution Theory." Learners can be trained to attribute their failures to causes other than ability; these would include factors such as lack of prerequisite skills or insufficient knowledge that can be changed through remediation or training. The idea is to move children closer to taking personal responsibility for their learning. Media producers will not have daily access to their audience as parents and teachers would, but they can embed these ideas through modeling, statements, and scenarios to help children understand that they can exercise some control over their learning outcomes, if they use choose.

Strategy 5: Timing of feedback. This strategy complements strategy 5 under "Success Opportunities": informative feedback. In addition to being informative and credible (not gratuitous praise), the feedback should be given immediately, if possible, after completion of a learning task. This strategy is just as important for helping a child assume personal responsibility as it is for creating success opportunities.

Strategy 6: Message design. Make sure the message design of your media product includes not only features that will engage the learner and make for an attractive presentation (as suggested in strategy 2 under "Success Opportunities," make it fun!), but also include features that will help the learner assimilate the new information. Think of what cognitive or learning aids you can give or suggest to your audience that will help internalize the content. Children will take more personal responsibility for their learning if they believe they have the tools (strategies) to work with. Read the Take 2 feature box for more information on message design.

What Is Message Design?

Barbara Grabowski (1991) proposes four concepts that relate to message design:

1. Message: It's what you as a media producer have to communicate to your audience.
2. Instruction and learning: Instruction happens outside the learner (what you produce) and learning happens inside the learner (as a result of their own cognitive processes, etc.).
3. Media: The media you select to deliver your message.
4. Message design: Combines elements of the first three into the design.

Grabowski relates message design to a blueprint. An instructional plan or "blueprint" encompasses the learning objectives and suggested teaching methods, but, like a blueprint for a house, it does not specify the finishing details. That is where message design comes in. There are two crucial aspects of message design: instruction and learning.

Message design for instruction involves the physical form of your message (e.g., the features of the medium you select and how you use them, such as visuals, interactivity, text placement, etc.). Since learning takes place inside the child, message design for learning involves planning for how you will help your audience utilize learning and cognitive strategies to help them make sense of the information you present. Examples include analogies, mnemonics, concept maps, diagrams, simulations, and so on. As a media producer, you must concern yourself with both these aspects of message design.

Strategy 7: Famous role models. Use role models in your media presentations who have taken control of their lives even in the face of adversity. Where possible and appropriate, include a famous person from the entertainment arena, politics, or sports who has faced a challenge and overcome it to accomplish notable things. The role model(s) must be able to project the enthusiasm and motivational qualities that allowed them to overcome obstacles. Such models could be either children or adults. While younger children may not be familiar with adult celebrities or political figures, you could use a fictional character who embodies the qualities you wish to project.

❗ Tips and Tactics

No Budget for Celebrities?

Having a project budget that affords the talent fees of one or more celebrities would be nice. But not having one doesn't mean you can't incorporate effective role models into your productions. An alternative to famous role models is using unknown actors or even real (unprofessional) kids as on-camera role models. Peer models can be very effective in motivating your audience, especially if your audience can readily identify with them.

Strategy 8: Peer modeling of coping strategies. Show peer models using cognitive and learning strategies to work through difficulties in achieving learning goals. This is one way to help your audience see the value of taking personal responsibility for learning. Research demonstrates that observing peer models can help children embrace similar goals.

Strategy 9: Sequencing. When developing for interactive learning environments, allow some flexibility for the learner to sequence the material herself, one aspect of a learner-controlled environment. Age and personality variables may influence success in a learner-controlled environment. A study by Arnone and Grabowski found that high-curiosity students performed better than low-curiosity students in an interactive learner-controlled environment overall, but that the youngest students (first graders) benefited most when there was an advisement component. There is an element of uncertainty in a learner-controlled environment, and high-curiosity children have a higher tolerance for uncertainty than low-curiosity children. Low-curiosity children may perform better when uncertainty is reduced, for example, by receiving suggestions for sequencing content. Media producers should be prepared to adapt the learning environment to best suit individual learners' needs.

Strategy 10: Alternative modes of showing competence. Provide alternative modes, if possible, for the children in your audience to demonstrate their competence or knowledge of the content presented. This not only addresses personal responsibility but also encourages intrinsic motivation, as you will see in the next chapter.

Developmental Snapshot
The Child at Nine

The nine-year-old continues to mature and enjoys social relationships more than ever. The good friends she made at eight years of age carry over, and friendships are increasingly important. She is still very curious but not quite as exuberant as a year ago; now, with her skills and knowledge growing dramatically, she can become more inner-directed. She does not need her parents for as many things, is very respectful of others, and expects the same from others. She has many outside activities and interests and is quite self-motivated. Although this is the beginning of the preadolescent phase, she keeps a healthy distance from the boys, as do the boys from her. They (the girls) don't care much how they (the boys) look, but she is more interested in her wardrobe these days. Her reading and mathematical abilities can be used for many practical purposes in her everyday life. She can become absorbed in chapter books for the inherent intrinsic satisfaction.

Note: Developmental snapshots are necessarily general and do not take into consideration wide variations in individual differences related to personality, learning, or physical development.

FINAL NOTE

This chapter covered many motivational principles and strategies that can be employed in the design of media for children in an effort to build their

BUILDING AND REINFORCING CONFIDENCE

confidence. Obviously not all strategies are appropriate for all situations, age-groups, or media. Yet you should be able to use the suggested strategies as a springboard in brainstorming ideas for your particular project(s) and specific motivational concerns.

COMING UP NEXT . . .

Have you provided enough intrinsic and extrinsic rewards? Do you feel that your audience will want to know more about the topic after viewing or interacting with your media product? How can you help children apply what they know to new situations? These and other questions will be answered in chapter 8 when we discuss the final ARCS component—satisfaction.

PRODUCER'S CHECKLIST

- ❏ Confidence is the third component of the ARCS model and contributes to the expectancy for success factor in expectancy-value theory.
- ❏ Confidence can be broken into three main categories:
  - Learning requirements
  - Success opportunities
  - Personal responsibility
- ❏ Self-efficacy relates to a child's perception of her abilities. Sometimes the perception and the actual abilities are different.
- ❏ Self-fulfilling prophecy is based on the notion that individuals will behave in a manner consistent with expectations others have of them.
- ❏ Attribution theory suggests that a person will attribute his successes and failures in learning tasks to one of four factors: ability, effort, task difficulty, and luck. Ability and effort are internal factors whereas as task difficulty and luck are external factors.
- ❏ Internal and external factors can be perceived in terms of a child's locus of control. A child with an internal locus of control, for example, is more likely to attribute his successes and failures to ability or effort.
- ❏ Learned helplessness often results from repeated failures. The child simply gives up trying.
- ❏ Attribution retraining attempts to train disappointed learners to attribute their failures to factors that are changeable (learning strategies, insufficient knowledge, etc.) rather than ability, a more stable factor.

- ❏ Message design incorporates four concepts: the message, instruction and learning, the media, and message design.
- ❏ Establishing learning goals is more effective than setting performance goals, especially for low-ability learners and learners lacking motivation.
- ❏ Strategies for addressing learning requirements include setting clear expectations and creating a nurturing learning environment.
- ❏ Strategies for promoting success opportunities include setting the right challenge, making the learning fun, and chunking information.
- ❏ Strategies for encouraging personal responsibility include equating success with effort, encouraging self-regulation and appraisal, and using peer models to demonstrate the use of learning strategies in working through problems.

DIGGING DEEPER

Arnone, Marilyn P., Grabowski, Barbara L., and Rynd, Christopher P. 1994. "Curiosity as a Personality Variable Influencing Learning in a Learner-Controlled Lesson with and without Advisement." *Educational Technology Research and Development* 42, no. 1: 5–20.

Bandura, A. 1986. *Social Foundations of Thought and Action: A Social-Cognitive Theory.* Englewood Cliffs, N.J.: Prentice-Hall.

Brophy, Jere. 1998. *Failure Syndrome Students*. ERIC Digest, ED419625.

———. 1989. "Synthesis of Research on Strategies for Motivating Students to Learn." *Educational Leadership,* October, 40–48.

Csikszentmihalyi, Mihaly. 1990. *Flow: The Psychology of Optimal Experience.* New York: Harper & Row.

Csikszentmihalyi, Mihaly, and Csikszentmihalyi, Isabella. 1988. *Optimal Experience: Psychological Studies of Flow in Consciousness.* Cambridge: Cambridge University Press.

Dohrn, Elizabeth, and Bryan, Tanis. 1994. "Attribution Instruction" *Teaching Exceptional Children* 26, no. 4: 61–63.

Dweck, Carol S. 1986. "Motivational Processes Affecting Learning." *American Psychologist* 41, no. 10: 1040–48.

Fishel, Catherine. 2001. *Designing for Children: Marketing Design That Speaks to Kids.* Gloucester, Mass.: Rockport.

Grabowski, Barbara. 1991. "Message Design: Issues and Trends." In Gary J. Anglin, ed., *Instructional Technology: Past, Present, and Future.* Englewood, Colo.: Libraries Unlimited.

Rosenthal, R., and Jacobson, L. 1968. *Pygmalion in the Classroom.* New York: Holt, Rinehart & Winston.

Rotter, Julian B. 1966. "Generalized Expectancies for Internal versus External Locus of Reinforcement." *Psychological Monographs* 80: 69.

Schunk, Dale H. 1996. *Self-efficacy for Learning and Performance.* American Educational Research Association.

Song, Sang H., and Keller, John M. 2001. "Effectiveness of Motivationally Adaptive Computer-Assisted Instruction on the Dynamic Aspects of Motivation." *Educational Technology Research and Development* 49, no. 2: 5–22.

Tauber, Robert T. 1998. *Good or Bad, What Teachers Expect from Students They Generally Get.* ERIC Digest, ED426985. www.ericsp.org/pages/digests/Good_or_bad.html.

Weiner, Bernard. 1980. *Human Motivation.* New York: Holt, Rinehart & Winston.

8

PROMOTING SATISFACTION (AND A CONTINUING MOTIVATION TO LEARN)

Satisfaction is the final component of Keller's ARCS model. Like confidence, satisfaction relates to the second factor of expectancy-value theory: expectancy for success. What is satisfying to one learner may not be to another. For some learners, the intrinsic satisfaction of learning something new is all that is required. For others, extrinsic incentives may be needed. Some believe that extrinsic incentives undermine a child's intrinsic motivation to learn. Others believe in a more balanced approach, agreeing that appropriate extrinsic incentives may help encourage intrinsic motivation. I support the latter view. In this chapter, we will explore satisfaction in detail, review several related motivational principles, and consider numerous strategies you can incorporate into your media product that will help accomplish the goal of promoting satisfaction and a continuing motivation to learn. Many of the constructs presented in chapter 7 also apply to satisfaction. Before I introduce the primary categories of strategies for the satisfaction component of the ARCS model, let's consider some of the motivational principles that underlie this component.

MOTIVATIONAL CONSTRUCTS RELATED TO SATISFACTION

Intrinsic Motivation

Intrinsic motivation, also known as self-motivation, is characterized by engaging in an activity purely for its own sake. Intrinsically motivated is what, ideally, we want learners to be—curious investigators exploring their world simply for the pleasure inherent in that exploration. Intrinsic motivation occurs when a child's drive for learning comes from within herself, usually instilled by an interest in the subject matter. Intrinsic motivation is closely related to academic achievement, a feeling of mastery, and a need for competence. In addition to presenting relevant and interesting content through the media we produce, we can encourage this type of motivation by providing intrinsic reinforcers such as opportunities to apply their new learning in a real situation soon after they achieve the learning goals, offering positive recognition, and providing additional information on topics of interest, just to name a few.

Looking back to your own experiences in childhood, you may recall that what was intrinsically motivating for you at one age changed as you grew older. As a child, I wanted to learn everything possible about horses and this intense interest lasted for several years. If I could wrap a school project around some aspect of horses, I was good to go. When it became apparent that my parents could never afford to buy me a horse, the motivation to read and absorb everything about them gradually waned and was replaced by some new interest. Intrinsic motivation is situational and can change over time. Moreover, what one child finds intrinsically motivating, another may not.

What constructs from chapter 7 do you suppose are also related to intrinsic motivation? One of them is flow theory. In a state of flow, you are intrinsically motivated to continue the activity in which you are engaged. Your interest, the optimal challenge level, immediate feedback, clear goals, and so on, all contribute to your intense involvement. Now think about locus of control (LOC). Would that also apply? Yes. Children with an internal LOC feel that they have more control over their learning, and this perception has been associated with intrinsic motivation. The results are more effort on tasks and a sense of competence that, in turn, influences intrinsic motivation. Finally, curiosity (discussed in chapter 5) also plays a role in intrinsic motivation and hence satisfaction. Curiosity is what motivates exploration; it is digging deeper because of a need to know. It is intrinsically motivated, and some have hypothesized that it is a natural precursor to flow.

❗ Tips and Tactics

Incentives: Strive for Balance!

Strive for balance in employing incentives that reward effort as well as ability and performance. Incentives that promote a sense of personal competence and accomplishment should be used as well as those that reward ability.

Extrinsic Motivation and Rewards

Extrinsic motivation comes from outside the individual and is not derived from the activity itself. You probably came by your share when you were in school; you know, the pizza party at the end of a big project, nifty stickers or gold stars on "A" papers, little trinkets for good behavior, and so on. As adults, we get lots of them, from our paychecks to promotions to store coupons that encourage us to buy things we really don't need, but we buy anyway because it's difficult to pass up the discount. Not receiving the rewards we expect often feels like punishment. So, the question is, are extrinsic rewards bad? The answer is no, if used judiciously.

By the dictionary's account, a reward is something given or obtained in return for work or services. Relating this to motivation, it places the sense of accomplishment outside of the student and so, in a sense, encourages an external LOC. Some research has suggested that extrinsic motivators given to children for a task that is intrinsically motivating to them may actually dampen their intrinsic motivation to engage in that task in the future. If the task is intrinsically motivating, there is no need for extrinsic incentives.

While some theorists oppose the use of extrinsic rewards, others feel that a balance between intrinsic and extrinsic motivators is the best solution. In fact, you may even be able to enhance intrinsic motivation by the proper use of extrinsic incentives. For example, a child who has not discovered the joy of reading is given an incentive to read. The child reads. The child discovers that she enjoys reading for pleasure. She no longer needs incentives to read.

Providing credible positive feedback is an extrinsic reward that increases a child's sense of competence and thus enhances intrinsic motivation. Extrinsic rewards that are tied to the learning task rather than unrelated to the task are also effective.

Media producers must necessarily be concerned with reaching the greatest number of children with their products. A good way to accommodate a large audience is to use a balance of extrinsic and intrinsic motivators embedded in the design.

Both intrinsic and extrinsic motivation contributes to the satisfaction component of the ARCS model.

THE SATISFACTION COMPONENT OF THE ARCS MODEL

The ARCS model includes three primary categories of strategies for building confidence:

- Intrinsic reinforcement
- Extrinsic rewards
- Equity

Each of these categories will be explained and applied to children's media with a number of examples and strategies.

INTRINSIC REINFORCEMENT

With what you know about intrinsic motivation, think about what children, who are intrinsically motivated, look like while engaged in a learning task. They are involved, seem to know clearly what is expected of them, demonstrate curiosity, appear to have an internal LOC as indicated by their effort, feel good about the challenge, and may even lose track of time. Building intrinsic reinforcement into the motivational design of your media project will help move your audience closer to being intrinsically motivated not only for the task at hand but toward learning in general.

Strategies for Stimulating Intrinsic Reinforcement

Strategy 1: Recognizing personal best. Encourage self-efficacy by recognizing when a learner makes an accomplishment due to effort or ability.

This can happen directly in an interactive learning environment or vicariously in a video or television scenario using principles of observational learning and modeling.

Strategy 2: Finished products (feeling of accomplishment). Promote a sense of accomplishment by having learners create a finished product making use of new learning. These may be suggestions put forth at the conclusion of a video or television program, or incorporated into a website.

Strategy 3: Information access. Promote the continuing motivation to learn about the topic of your presentation by providing access to additional information after viewing your video or interacting with your website. Information access can be via Web, print, or recommendations on where to find more information. Pave the way for their continued exploration and tell them how they might use what they have learned in another context.

Strategy 4: Assessment options. Allow learners to choose how they will be evaluated. Include options for projects, presentations, portfolios, and so on, in addition to more formal tests and quizzes. If your media product is only one component of a total learning package, work with curriculum developers to decide how to best evaluate the learning from your product in the context of the whole curriculum.

Strategy 5: Learning orientation. Help children move toward a learning orientation rather than just an evaluation orientation. Use role models to suggest a love of learning for its own sake, demonstrate the fun of being curious, and the satisfaction of exploring and then resolving the question that curiosity induced.

Strategy 6: Verbal or textual reinforcement tied to intrinsic motivation. Use verbal reinforcement in video and interactive media to reinforce the child's intrinsic satisfaction and sense of competence on achieving a goal or subgoal. Acknowledge what was necessary for achievement to happen.

Strategy 7: Parental involvement. Get parents involved in your project through your website or print support materials. For example, have a parents' section of your site in which you provide information about parental influences in a child's intrinsic motivation to learn. Provide some strategies they can use at home to encourage this type of motivation. For video producers, you can add a print support piece just for parents that is an insert to the video. You can do the same if your product is for school distribution but aim your support at classroom teachers.

The Research Says...

When parents use reward strategies for children's school accomplishments that emphasize *competence*, they positively affect their children's intrinsic motivation to learn. Media producers can help parents understand this important strategy through incorporating this information in video, television, or Web support materials directed to parents (Gottfried and Gottfried 2001).

EXTRINSIC REWARDS

Be aware of the potential for declining intrinsic motivation by the improper use of extrinsic rewards. How would you recognize such an outcome in a child? You might notice that the same activity he used to enjoy purely for its own sake doesn't seem as interesting anymore. He may stop doing it, unless there is some tangible reward for doing so. Rewards that are unrelated to the learning situation do nothing to instill an appreciation for lifelong learning. Related rewards, on the other hand, can be very useful. As mentioned earlier in this chapter, a balance that includes both intrinsic reinforcement and extrinsic rewards works best.

Strategies for Providing Extrinsic Rewards

Strategy 1: Positive feedback. Provide positive feedback when small goals are attained. Especially when students are learning something new, feedback should be frequent. Interactive media can provide praise for correct responses. As learners become more competent, this type of feedback should be periodic to conserve its effectiveness.

Strategy 2: Games. Use noncompetitive games in interactive learning systems to provide feedback during the learning process. This can be fun and satisfying when a child is measuring himself against a personal achievement goal.

Strategy 3: Recognition based on accomplishment. Provide recognition for accomplishment. In a Web component of a television program I coproduced, we established a Hall of Frames, a virtual gallery where children could display their artistic creations after working on them while viewing the television program. They could mail them to us or scan them and upload them to the site. Let children know at the end of your video or television program, if possible, that there is an outlet for them to showcase their accomplishments.

Strategy 4: Related rewards. Provide rewards that relate to or reinforce the learning from your media presentation. On a website we produced to teach evaluation skills to children in the primary grades, we gave them informational coloring pages they could download. This is a low-cost/low-tech reward, but effective. The coloring pages included additional brief informational snippets on the content presented on the site.

Strategy 5: Symbolic rewards. Provide symbolic rewards for accomplishment. Children who complete and submit a related task after viewing a video or television program, or participate in an interactive learning event, can be mailed or e-mailed a special certificate recognizing their achievement.

EQUITY

Equity in Keller's model refers to fairness and consistency. For a child to realize his expectation for success, the media producer and team must make certain that there is consistency between the objectives of the project as presented to the audience, and how they measure whether the audience has achieved success.

Strategies for Promoting a Sense of Equity

Strategy 1: Consistency. Make sure your evaluation fairly represents the content you have presented. If you plan to test learners on the content, it should be at the same level as presented. While this sounds like a no-brainer, you would be surprised at how often children are expected to demonstrate knowledge or skills that go beyond what they could have acquired from a media presentation alone.

Strategy 2: Amount of work. Require an appropriate amount of work to demonstrate knowledge of the content presented, neither more nor less than is necessary.

Strategy 3: Fairness. If your media project involves a testing component, make certain that the criteria for assessment are equal for all children involved.

Remember that your audience motivational analysis will help you determine which strategies and how many are appropriate for your target audience. The delimitations of your media platform will also influence your strategy decisions. Now let's take a peek at another developmental snapshot—the child at ten, a really great age!

**Developmental Snapshot
The Child at Ten**

The ten-year-old has a great deal of experience under his belt from home to school and the community. He accepts himself and, more importantly, feels good about himself. He "knows how to act" in most situations and gets along well with peers and teachers. He enjoys being with his parents and participating in family activities, and can be very affectionate. Parents love this age. Intellectually, he is at the point where he can see several sides of an issue, reads well, can do fairly complex mathematical problems, and has the ability to strategize when he wants. He still does not want much to do with the opposite sex and is still unscathed from those tumultuous teen years that lie ahead. He loves participating in lots of activities, many of which are of his own design. Does this snapshot give you any ideas of strategies you might use to motivate the ten-year-old?

Note: Developmental snapshots are necessarily general and do not take into consideration wide variations in individual differences related to personality, learning, or physical development.

FINAL NOTE

You have now learned the final two components of the ARCS model that address the expectation for success factor of expectancy-value theory—confidence and satisfaction (see figure 5). You have also discovered some practical strategies for addressing these components with a child audience in a media-related project.

```
┌─────────────────────────┐
│  EXPECTANCY for SUCCESS │
└─────────────────────────┘
            │
     ┌──────┴──────┐
┌─────────┐  ┌──────────────┐
│Confidence│  │ Satisfaction │
└─────────┘  └──────────────┘
```

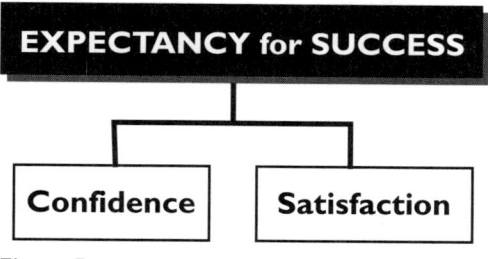

Figure 5.

Now that you are familiar with all the ARCS model components, I have my own suggestion (or strategy) designed to stimulate your continuing motivation to learn. Here it is. Perhaps you might find it interesting to do your own mini media research project. This would help you practice using your knowledge of the ARCS model and broaden your knowledge of what is currently in the television marketplace. Consider conducting a content analysis of existing children's television programs, using the ARCS model. A content analysis breaks down or delineates program elements in order to discern characteristics that might contribute, for example, to program appeal or other factor such as comprehension, and so on. We are interested in the motivational elements for this research project. Here is what to do.

Select a sample of programs to review; include several popular programs for children in the age-group you are targeting and several less known or less popular programs. Watch every segment. Create an ARCS matrix that allows you to categorize any motivational strategies being used throughout the program. Analyze your data, noting which programs used which ARCS strategies and how often. Is there any pattern that you can detect?

COMING UP NEXT . . .

In chapter 9, we will briefly explore how the motivational aspects of your television and video products can converge nicely with your associated Web product. You will also see how you can measure the effectiveness of that convergence. Finally, we will briefly consider the importance of Web accessibility as it pertains to motivation, and several television and Web laws for children that you should be aware of.

PRODUCER'S CHECKLIST

- ❏ Satisfaction is the final component of the ARCS model; like confidence, it also relates to the expectancy for success factor in expectancy-value theory.
- ❏ Several of the constructs discussed in previous chapters also apply to satisfaction. They include flow, locus of control, and curiosity.
- ❏ Intrinsic motivation occurs when a child is motivated to engage in an activity or learning task for the pure enjoyment of it. It is motivation that comes from within.
- ❏ Extrinsic motivation comes from external factors that influence a child's motivation to learn, such as rewards.
- ❏ When used in balance with intrinsic reinforcers, extrinsic rewards can be effective in motivating your audience.
- ❏ The ARCS model suggests three main categories of strategies for satisfaction:
    - Intrinsic reinforcement
    - Extrinsic rewards
    - Equity
- ❏ Strategies for intrinsic reinforcement include recognition of a child's achievement of her personal best and access to additional information on the topic in order to promote a continuing motivation to learn.
- ❏ Strategies related to extrinsic rewards include positive feedback and symbolic rewards.
- ❏ Strategies to promote equity include consistency and fairness.

DIGGING DEEPER

Arnone, M. P., and Small, Ruth V. 1995. "Arousing and Sustaining Curiosity: Lessons from the ARCS Model." In *17th Annual Proceedings of Selected Research and Development Presentations,* National Convention of the Association for Educational Communications and Technology (Anaheim, Calif.), 1–15.

Gottfried, Adele E., and Gottfried, Allen W. 1991. *Parents' Reward Strategies and Children's Academic Intrinsic Motivation and School Performance.* ERIC Digest, ED335144.

Ingram, Michael A. 2000. *Extrinsic Motivators and Incentives: Challenge and Controversy.* ERIC Digest, ED448127.

Institute of Academic Excellence. 1997. *Toward a Balanced Approach to Reading Motivation: Resolving the Intrinsic-Extrinsic Rewards Debate.* ERIC Digest, ED421687.

Keller, J. M. 1983. "Motivational Design of Instruction." In C. M. Reigeluth, ed., *Instructional Design Theories and Models: An Overview of Their Current Status.* Hillsdale, N.J.: Erlbaum.

Rotto, Luther. 1994. "Curiosity, Motivation and 'Flow' in Computer-Based Instruction." Paper presented at the annual conference of the Association for Educational Communications and Technology, Nashville.

9

GUIDELINES, MANDATES, AND CONSIDERATIONS FOR CONVERGENCE MEDIA

Part 2 concludes with a few important considerations for developing children's media and a practical producer's tool. These include:

- Accessible Web design
- The Children's Online Privacy Protection Act
- The Children's Television Act
- Convergence media
- A kids-based evaluation tool for convergence media

ACCESSIBLE WEB DESIGN

The World Wide Web, with all its potential for providing rich learning environments, multimedia, and powerful means for organizing information through hyperlinks, suffers tremendously because it lacks universal compliance. Multiple browsers, poor Web design, lack of attention to standards for presentation and structure all contribute to the problem. Who suffers most from this? Users who have visual, auditory, or other physical disabilities, users with older or different browsers or slow Internet connections, and users who speak a language other than that in which the Web page was written may suffer from lack of attention to universal design principles.

The World Wide Web Consortium (W3C) has developed accessibility guidelines that will help ensure that all persons, regardless of their disability, assistive technology used, or outdated equipment, can enjoy the great resource offered by the Web. These guidelines are compliant with the Americans with Disabilities Act (ADA) and the Assistive Technology Act of 1998. The guidelines were produced as part of the Web Accessibility Initiative (WAI) and you can find them by visiting the W3C website: www.w3.org and selecting the Accessibility link from the home page . There you will discover handy checklists organized by priorities.

It is fairly easy to meet priority 1 and many of the priority 2 checkpoints that enable some groups of users to access your site with ease. Several of the guidelines you will find include providing text equivalents for nontext elements such as images and other graphics, making backgrounds with sufficient contrast in the foreground to help persons with color deficits or black and white monitors, and using style sheets to control presentation and layout. Let's say you plan to incorporate a number of videos in your Web project. Consider that some users who are blind may use a speech output system that allows screen text to be read aloud. How could you use videos but still accommodate this sector of your audience? One way is to offer transcriptions of each video. You might also consider auditory descriptions. For hearing-impaired children of reading age, you could caption your videos. Audio clips should also be transcribed.

Following universal design principles can have a positive impact on motivation. Think back to expectancy-value theory and the ARCS model as we consider the following examples.

- Several of the (WAI) guidelines have to do with the organization of a website. These refer to the ability of persons to easily navigate the site and find the information they desire. Consistent placement of the menu bar, organizational cues that give users a clear sense of where they are at all times, a site map, and easy access to help aids are just a few ways to enhance organization. The W3C also recommends dividing large blocks of information into "more manageable groups where natural and appropriate." A well-organized site contributes to the user's expectancy for success and that naturally relates to confidence.
- Maintaining the currency and accuracy of your site requires regular updating and supervision. This also adds to the value of your site by increasing its relevance. Providing information "so that users may re-

ceive documents according to their preferences," also recommended in the WAI guidelines, increases value and relevance, as well.

Don't forget to visit the W3C site mentioned earlier for greater detail on accessible Web design as well as links to sources where you can put your design to the test to see if it is truly accessible.

! Tips and Tactics

Know Your Audience!

Again, audience analysis is critical. You must understand their needs and plan for them in the design of your website. How will different members of your audience experience your Web page? Test your Web page under different conditions. Employing universal design principles will allow your Web page to be successfully accessed by the widest possible audience.

THE CHILDREN'S ONLINE PRIVACY PROTECTION ACT

On April 21, 2000, the Children's Online Privacy Protection Act (COPPA) went into effect enforced by the Federal Trade Commission (FTC). As a children's media producer, you must be aware of and comply with the requirements of this act that is designed to protect the privacy rights of children under the age of 13. To comply with COPPA, you must state the privacy protection policy on the homepage and at every point where information about the child could be collected. The content of the privacy policy must include what information about the child will be collected, how it will be used, whether it will be made available to third parties, that the resources of the site may be used without disclosing information, and various rights of the parent and child. There must also be a direct notice to parents and verifiable parental consent. While COPPA does not relate specifically to motivation, as a producer of children's media, you need to become familiar with this federal mandate. To find out more, visit the kids privacy section of the FTC site online at www.ftc.gov/kidzprivacy.

Watch Out!

Don't use words that children cannot understand. Use examples whenever possible to help convey the meaning of your website's privacy policy.

THE CHILDREN'S TELEVISION ACT

The Children's Television Act (CTA) was enacted by Congress in 1990. While its purpose was to mandate television stations in the United States under the Federal Communications Commission (FCC) to serve the educational and informational (E/I) needs of children by providing core educational programming, it was somewhat vague. Some station operators failed to comply according to the meaning of the CTA, claiming to fulfill their obligations with programming that clearly did not serve the E/I needs of children in the manner intended by the mandate. Consequently in 1996 the FCC adopted new rules to bolster and enforce the CTA to go into effect in January 1997. Television stations now had clearer definitions of what programs qualified as "core" programs, as well as acceptable program lengths and scheduling requirements. Television stations had to air at least three hours per week of regularly scheduled core programs for children between the hours of 7:00 A.M. and 10:00 P.M. Previously some stations had been airing programs before 7:00 A.M., when children were unlikely to watch. The FCC also adopted a number of initiatives to help parents acquire more information about the core programs being aired by their local stations. Complying with the CTA is a condition of television broadcast station license renewal, thus ensuring that broadcasters take this mandate seriously. They must complete quarterly reports on what they have done to address the E/I needs of children and make their reports available to the public.

For more information on the CTA, visit the FCC children's educational television Web page at www.fcc.gov/mb/policy/kidstv.html. Child advocacy, health, and educational organizations have since called on the FCC to further strengthen the CTA and reporting by broadcasters. Recently some legislators have drawn attention to how children can be better served as digital technology continues to develop, asking child advocates to question how the CTA might be interpreted in a digital multicast environment. I think it is safe to say that the Children's Television Act will continue to evolve as time goes on.

CONVERGENCE MEDIA

The term "convergence media" refers to bringing together various forms of media in a synergetic manner. The idea of convergence media has been bandied about since the mid-1990s but has been realized only recently. It is more than just the idea of a television set outfitted with a device for high-speed interconnectivity or the opportunity to hit a buy button while watching an infomercial on television. More than simply a leap in technical capability, it is an expanded way of thinking about media that will continue to be an important consideration in developing children's media.

How will the television program translate to its Web counterpart? How can you maximize the interactivity strengths of the Web to balance the passive nature of linear television or video? If your television program is financed in part by the marketing of its inherent products, how can the Web be used to cross-promote your products? Will interactive television ever be able to blend the strengths of the Internet, in terms of e-commerce and ability for a customized interactive experience, with the power of television and video as dramatic entertainment mediums? These are just a few of the questions that producers must ask of themselves in today's marketplace.

Convergence media exists in varying degrees of complexity from the simple website that expands or reinforces the content presented in a video or television series to the program that depends on the Web as a critical component. For example, remember *Star Search?* Kids, teenagers, and parents alike watched the television program featuring new talent and then hurried to vote for their favorites on the Web. The results were tallied and winners announced. Yes, it was primitive from a technological perspective but still effective. Audience participation was enthusiastic and it definitely contributed to viewers' motivation to watch the series.

Some television programs simply add a URL to the bottom of the frame letting you know where you can find out more information on the topic presented. This is technically unsophisticated but can be an inexpensive, effective manner of converging media for some programs. Some broadcasters feared viewers would jump out of their seats and head for the computer, while others simply expected that viewers would write down the information and find out more after viewing the program. You can be sure that the advertising community is actively pursuing research on this topic to shed light on viewers' actual behaviors. Fears of losing viewers to the computer work station will disappear, and viewers will be able to do it all without moving from their comfortable sofas or favorite TV chairs. Viewers, including our younger ones, want and expect opportunities for higher-caliber media participation, including actually being inside the television or video environments experiencing the adventures, calling the shots, making decisions that will affect the outcomes of their favorite programs—at least virtually. This scenario will demand that technology and creativity intersect at a much higher level. Producers will be challenged like never before. Marketers will have to find new ways of selling products, perhaps embedding them in the adventures themselves. And the costs initially will be tremendous to create both the technical infrastructure and the appropriate content. So, for now, let's return to earth and consider another example of effectively converging media that creative producers even on low budgets can accomplish. . . .

A basic yet effective example of a print–Web convergence project is the Ghost Hunter series of books written by Trish Kline for nine- to eleven-year-olds. Each book includes interactive "webscenes." At various points throughout the story, the reader is instructed to visit a specific Web link that contains an image, a puzzle, or another piece of information critical to the story. Alternatively, video producers could produce video vignettes to accompany a storybook. Along the same vein, I am currently creating a DVD/book series featuring curious kids to promote information literacy skills and curiosity.

By the time this book is released, there will be further technical advances and new ideas for maximizing the potential of convergent media. What you have learned about motivation and strategies for instilling it, however, will remain constant and will give you an edge in developing media for children regardless of how quickly and radically the technology unfolds. Along with such advances comes a responsibility for creators of children's media. We must be mindful of the potential effects on their cognitive, physical and socio-behavioral development. More research will be needed. In May 2004, the Children and Media Research Advancement Act (CAMRA) was introduced by Senators Lieberman, Brownback, and Clinton. The purpose of the CAMRA Act would be to research the role and impact that electronic media has on children. In the bill, Congress acknowledges that there are "important gaps in our knowledge of electronic media and in particular, the newer interactive digital media in children's healthy development." The bill would amend the Public Health Service Act and provide substantial research funding to the National Institute of Child Health and Human Development. I am certain there will be more developments on this by the time you read this chapter.

Developmental Snapshot
The Child at Eleven

The child between the ages of eleven and twelve undergoes many changes physically and emotionally. She is at the cusp of adolescence and with that comes both a growth surge and some degree of turmoil. At times, she may be loud, moody, extremely sensitive, or confrontational with both friends and family as she struggles to become her own person. She finds it increasingly difficult to concentrate, especially on school, perhaps because she is beginning to show more interest in the opposite sex. The social aspects of school overshadow the learning opportunities. Friends continue to be key in her social development process and loyalty is expected at all times. In terms of media entertainment, she wants to learn more about herself and her world, gravitating toward real-life and factual programs as opposed to fantasy.

Note: Developmental snapshots are necessarily general and do not take into consideration wide variations in individual differences related to personality, learning, or physical development.

A KIDS-BASED EVALUATION TOOL FOR CONVERGENCE MEDIA

WebMAC for Children's TV Websites

WebMAC for Children's TV Websites is based on the original Website Motivational Analysis Checklist (WebMAC) Junior-2000, which was designed to be used as an educational tool providing children with hands-on experience in evaluating the strengths and weaknesses of World Wide Web sites. It was pilot-tested with 500 students in Bucks County, Pennsylvania, revised, and published in *WWW Motivation Mining: Finding Treasures for Teaching Evaluation Skills, Grades 1–6*.

The tool presented in this book evolved because of the convergence of television programs and the World Wide Web and a TV/Web project that my company was commissioned to evaluate. Instead of being used to teach evaluation skills, this tool helped guide the user-based design of the website in focus groups with children. Because it proved useful to me, I am sharing it with the readers of this book. If you make copies of the tool for your own use as a producer, please provide credit to the authors as listed in "Digging Deeper" at the end of this chapter.

Description and Purpose

WebMAC for Children's TV Websites is a tool for producers and designers working on convergence media projects to assess the motivational quality of a website (with a television program counterpart) from a child's perspective. The version here is targeted for eight- to eleven-year-old children but is easily modifiable up or down. While it is designed for Web/TV convergence, it can easily be modified for Web/video should you be developing a website to support, for example, a video series offered through schools or other marketing venues. The instrument includes twenty-eight items that can be measured quantitatively plus several questions that can be used as a springboard for a follow-up interview or focus group; it can also be analyzed qualitatively.

Theoretical Background

This instrument focuses on the motivational aspects of a website while other Web-based evaluation instruments often focus on technical or functionality issues. As you already know, motivation answers the why of behavior. Applying motivation to websites generates the following questions:

- Why visit?
- Why stay?
- Why return?

Websites associated with children's television programs can easily address the first question by "promotion." Such websites are often cross-promoted on the television program itself, sometimes including the URL in the credits. In addition, they are promoted in other materials such as newsletters, advertisements, and so on. But how do you know your website keeps visitors interested enough to continue browsing the site, motivates visitors to take an interest in program-related products or services should they become available, keeps visitors coming back, and inspires children to recommend the site to other children? These were the questions that motivated the development of this evaluation instrument.

As mentioned earlier, the purpose of the instrument is to assess the motivational quality of a children's TV website from the child's perspective. The instrument is based on a solid foundation of research in the field of motivation. Since you are already familiar with expectancy-value theory and the ARCS model, the structure of the instrument should make excellent sense to you. The research concepts as applied to online experience suggest that a child will be motivated to remain at a website if:

1. The site has value (meaningfulness) to him or her AND
2. The child has the expectation of succeeding in the website environment.

Both value and expectation for success must be present for a child to be positively engaged in a particular website and be motivated to return to it. The degree to which these qualities are present in a website designed for a specific group of child users constitutes the motivational rating of the site. Consider the following as a review of what you have learned in earlier chapters as applied specifically to a child's online experience.

What contributes to the value and success aspects of a child's website (or any website)? As you know, John Keller in his well-documented and widely implemented ARCS model of motivational design suggests that strategies designed to increase attention (A) and relevance (R) contribute to the value component while strategies designed to increase confidence (C) and satisfaction (S) contribute to the expectation for success component.

Attention strategies include elements that capture and sustain interest and curiosity beginning with the first impressions created by the homepage. Relevance relates to the usefulness, credibility, and appropriateness of the site for the designated audience. Children will visit a TV website if they like or are interested in the TV program itself. While the website is a great opportunity to expand on the learning and entertainment opportunities of its television counterpart, it will lose relevance if it deviates too much from the look and feel that children know from the television program. Ease of navigation, shared control, friendly information and interface design, and clarity translate to confidence-building elements. Opportunities for interaction, exploration, fun, and competency translate to a satisfying experience. With this in mind, see if you can recognize which of the following items relate to value or expectancy for success. (The items are not in the same sequence as on the actual instrument.)

1. How easy was it to find your way around without getting lost?
2. Were there enough characters from the TV show at this website?
3. Did you learn anything that you didn't learn from the TV show?
4. Did all the parts of this website work the way they should?

You are correct if you associated items 1 and 4 with expectancy for success and items 2 and 3 with value. For example, item 2 is a value item because it addresses relevance; were there no characters from the TV show on the website, it would lack relevance and affect the value subscore.

You will find the complete administrator directions and scoring guidelines for WebMAC for Children's TV Websites in appendix A and the children's evaluation instrument in appendix B.

COMING UP NEXT . . .

In part 3, we explore a case study in which both the ARCS model and the CTW model were employed in the creation of a children's television program that ran for more than six years on The Learning Channel.

PRODUCER'S CHECKLIST

❏ Accessible Web design ensures that individuals with visual or hearing impairments, those using assistive technologies, and users with slow Internet connections or older equipment can process the information available to them on the World Wide Web. The W3C oversees the Web Accessibility Initiative and offers guidelines for accessible Web design.
❏ All producers/developers of Web resources for children must include a privacy policy that clearly articulates how the privacy rights of child visitors are protected. This is called COPPA, or the Children's Online Privacy Protection Act.
❏ The Children's Television Act was originally enacted in 1990 and strengthened in 1996. Broadcast stations must meet the educational/informational needs of the child audience as a condition of television broadcast license renewal.

❑ Today, almost every children's television program has a Web counterpart. Convergence media adds a dimension of responsibility for children's media producers as well as enhanced opportunities for development of synergetic media experiences for children.
❑ The WebMAC TV tool described in this chapter and included in the appendixes can be used in the design and/or evaluation phase(s) of producing a website based on a children's television program. One way of utilizing the instrument is by incorporating a user-based design approach in child-centered focus groups. It can also be utilized as an evaluation tool once the site is up and running to assess its ongoing effectiveness across motivational variables that impact children's adoption of a website.

DIGGING DEEPER

Arnone, Marilyn P., and Small, Ruth V. 2003. *Website Motivational Analysis Checklist (WebMAC) for Children's Television Web Sites.* (See appendix.)
———. 1999. *WWW Motivation Mining: Finding Treasures for Teaching Evaluation Skills, Grades 1–6.* Worthington, Ohio: Linworth.
Benton Foundation. 1996. *Children's Television Programming: The FCC Gives Teeth to the Children's Television Act of 1990.* www.benton.org/Policy/TV/kidstvsum.html.
Congress 108th. May 19, 2004. *Children and Media Research Advancement Act (CAMRA Act).* Bill No. S. 2447.
Federal Communications Commission (FCC). *Children's Educational Television.* www.fcc.gov/mb/policy/kidstv.html. (accessed 7/21/04)
Federal Communications Commission. 1996. *Revision of Programming Policies for Television Broadcast Stations.* FCC 96-335.
Federal Trade Commission Web Site (FTC). *Kidz Privacy: Just for Kids.* www.ftc.gov/bcp/conline/edcams/kidzprivacy/kidz.htm. (accessed 7/21/04)
Keller, John. 1999. "Motivation in Cyber Learning Environments." *International Journal of Educational Technology* 1, no. 1: 7–30.
Lynch, Patrick J., and Horton, Sarah. 2001. *Web Style Guide: Basic Design Principles for Creating Web Sites.* 2d ed. New Haven: Yale University Press.
Sprague, Carolyn Ann. 1999. *Accessible Web Design.* ERIC Digest, EDO-IR-1999-09. www.ericit.org/digests/EDO-IR-1999-09.shtml.

Part 3

USING THE CTW AND ARCS MODELS TO REDESIGN A CHILDREN'S TV PROGRAM (A CASE STUDY)

10

A LOCAL PHENOMENON

Part 3 of this book takes you through a case study showing you how the two models, CTW and ARCS, were used to redesign an existing television program for children. Why am I selecting this particular case study? Because of its highs and lows. I believe that it exemplifies the real need for an integrated approach to children's programming. This case study takes you behind the scenes for a look at the consequences of neglecting to implement a solid educational plan and targeted motivational strategies; it also explores the turnaround achieved once a good plan was in place. This chapter provides a brief background on the project.

HUMBLE BEGINNINGS

It started as a local public access program in Syracuse, New York. By anyone's standards, it was very, very low budget with little or no production value. Yet the program's character, Pappy, a friendly old codger with a bent hat, sparkling eyes, a bright scarf around his neck, suspenders, and a huge pencil slung over his shoulder, had a special charm that the local audience loved. He had charm and he had talent, lots of it. Pappy Drew-it was an artist and every week he invited the local kids to draw along with him. The results were incredible; kids were drawing and having a ball. No fancy gimmicks, no fast cuts; just honest participation and Pappy Drew-it gently guiding his audience through their paces. He made personal appearances and the kids showed up in droves. For the first time, this town had a children's celebrity in its midst.

NEXT STEP

Others noticed this local phenomenon and wondered if, given an influx of capital, some real sets and higher production value, plus a supporting cast, the show would sell on a national level. The Children's Television Act was now a reality, and television stations needed to prove that their children's programs were meeting the educational needs of their young audiences. Consequently the producers were anxious to have educational input. The executive producer called me, and we discussed the program and its potential. I knew of the phenomenal local following that Pappy enjoyed and felt he had something very special to share. So I agreed to write an educational prospectus of sorts, describing the potential for the program to provide an outlet for children's drawing and creative expression, tied to a program theme that addressed pro-social values and life skills. All this took place before series production and was part of the effort to raise funding. My educational prospectus was used in every funding proposal and meeting to show potential investors how much educational integrity the program would have. That said, the other and most important issue for investors was the potential return on investment (ROI). The ROI would come in the form of marketing Pappy products, a common method with most children's programs these days.

Funding was acquired to produce twenty-six episodes of the show, to be called *Pappyland*. A production studio in western New York State was contracted. Sets were built—both full-size and miniatures, puppets (support cast) were created, a fully orchestrated theme song was recorded, an on-camera songster/musician was hired, and a production crew assembled. I waited for a call that the program executives were ready for my services to help guide the educational direction of the program. I was ready. But I didn't get the call. Eventually a call came, but the scripts had already been written and the crew was "ready to roll." I think they just wanted me to take a quick look and give my stamp of approval. I wasn't impressed. These guys were so anxious to get into the studio and crank out these episodes that they neglected a critical part of the puzzle—the educational viability of the program. The initial prospectus I had written only described the "potential" of the program. That potential could only be realized if a concerted effort were made to support both the educational and motivational goals of the program. I won't say the program's producers did not have good intentions.

It was simply the same old story from the pre-CTW days when "the broadcasters" didn't want their creativity to be hampered by "the educators." You would have thought that the CTW success story would have changed all that, but obviously some didn't get the message.

A FLAGSHIP STATION

It was decided that *Pappyland* should be broadcast on PBS commercial-free. That meant it needed a sponsoring station, often referred to as the flagship station. Based on the promise of the program, a major PBS affiliate in New York City agreed to be that station. With everything in place, studio production began and all twenty-six episodes were produced.

I can't tell you about how it went in the studio (because I wasn't there), but I can tell you that no educational consultants helped guide program decisions. There was no plan for formative evaluation, and I didn't hear from the producers during production. I figured my part was over; I wrote the prospectus, and that was that.

Scripting the educational message for each episode was done in the old-fashioned "fly by the seat of your pants with good intentions but no real knowledge of the child audience" approach. One of the episodes was titled "Loss." Prior to viewing the episode, I thought that the writer must have taken on the challenge of addressing a very serious topic. I wondered what direction the plot took in that episode. Did one of the characters lose a family member? Or perhaps a cherished pet? No. One of the characters lost his, well, toothbrush. (I guess it was a very special toothbrush.) Even a teddy bear would have worked better than a toothbrush in approaching this delicate concept! While the sets were great and Pappy was still very charming and talented, the show was stilted and lacked pacing. It was very, very slow.

What do you think happened when the New York City flagship station took a gander at the *Pappyland* episodes? You guessed it. . . . In a nutshell, they said "No way!" They feared, with good reason, the backlash the show would receive for not living up to serious educational scrutiny. The fact that the hoped-for flagship station declined to play the intended role was a huge setback.

ANOTHER ATTEMPT

Eventually the local PBS affiliate in Syracuse, New York, decided to sponsor the program. However, news soon came that the program wasn't doing well in terms of carriage (the number of stations airing it). While the program was broadcast on a number of PBS affiliates scattered throughout the country, most station program managers felt it had serious shortcomings. Eventually the original series aired on approximately 20 percent of PBS stations nationwide.

COMING UP NEXT ...

Can you see any hope for this floundering entity? It has a good program concept overall, an excellent principal talent in "Pappy," the drawing and creativity elements that kids love. Yet the show isn't going to fly, as is. Maybe a *Pappyland* makeover would help. That's the subject of chapter 11, "Rescue Efforts."

PRODUCER'S CHECKLIST

- ❏ Pappyland was selected as a case study because of the challenges it presents and the opportunities for improvement.
- ❏ Pappyland began as a local public access program in central New York with its character, Pappy Drew-it, quickly becoming a local children's celebrity.
- ❏ Seeing the potential, a group of investors prepared to produce twenty-six episodes with a full set, miniatures, and a cast of supporting characters.
- ❏ While an educational prospectus was commissioned to demonstrate the educational potential of the program, no attempt was made to actively engage educational consultants in the design of individual episodes.
- ❏ The New York City PBS station that had indicated it would serve as the "flagship" station for the series declined to play that role after viewing the completed episodes of *Pappyland*, fearing it would not live up to educational scrutiny.
- ❏ While another PBS station agreed to sponsor the program, it didn't get the acceptance from PBS affiliates that it had hoped for.

11

RESCUE EFFORTS

This chapter describes a successful effort to revive a floundering property. The outcome was a program that aired from 1996 until 2003 in first run and reruns on The Learning Channel (TLC). *TV Guide* rated the revived series as one of the top ten new children's programs in the country in 1996. The feature entitled "Top 10 New Kids' Shows" began, "Out of the season's 40-plus new kids' shows, we found a few that are smart, original, or just plain cool enough to really stand out." An excerpt from the feature follows.

An Excerpt from *TV Guide*

A drawing show that began in 1990 as a Syracuse public-access program, *Pappyland* (The Learning Channel, weekdays, 7:30 and 10:00 A.M./ET) is the antithesis of today's hyperactive style of TV. Instead, this series (which also airs on some PBS stations) inspires children to draw in an innocent, unhurried fashion. . . .

Twinkly, 40-something Michael Cariglio is the backwoods Pappy, a gray-bearded yet bright-eyed codger who gets kids scribbling, aided by a host of puppet sidekicks like Binky the Brush and Doodlebug. One major drawing per show is outlined and colored while the viewing audience follows along, and each picture relates to the episode's theme, such as friendship. Pappy takes his time sketching figures and filling them in with crayons, and his cartoonlike images are easy for home viewers to replicate. Throughout, the cheery cabin-dweller urges kids to indulge their own ideas about form and color. At the end, Pappy exhibits pictures sent in by viewers to date, some 47,000 pieces. A show that fosters creativity and participation? You can't beat that with a hickory stick.

—Moira McCormick, *TV Guide,* October 26–November 1, 1996, p. 41

The rest of the chapter details the journey to this new and improved program described by *TV Guide*.

A NEW DIRECTION

My business partner in Creative Media Solutions, MariRae Dopke, and I were asked to take over the production effort for *Pappyland*. While the owners of the program and its investors were a separate company, ours would become the production company of record. We decided we would take on the challenge. As part of the agreement, we were given full latitude for developing and implementing an educational plan and motivational goals. Program executives had some reservations on this score (the same broadcaster fears that educational input means creative disaster), but they agreed, knowing that lack of educational effort was one of the prime reasons the first twenty-six episodes were not acceptable by PBS standards. In fact, one of the challenges would be regaining the credibility lost to the lack of educational viability in the first twenty-six episodes.

Program redesign would necessitate not only addressing the educational aspects of the program but also improving the overall production value, crucial to achieving the motivational goals we would soon establish.

WHERE DO WE BEGIN?

Since this is a case study that is being used to exemplify the integration of the CTW and ARCS models, I would like you to revisit the integration concept back in chapter 4 on page 139 and then consider for yourself what the first steps should be.

FRONT-END ANALYSIS

The first step, of course, was front-end analysis. Our purpose was to hone in and identify both the pluses and the minuses of the existing property, plan the new programming effort, conduct an audience motivational analysis, address budget issues, make some decisions on how the revised effort would flow in terms of timelines, and so on. Our first meetings included the new executive producer, Eric Roberts, who was extremely creative and receptive to fresh ideas (the original program owners ran out of capital and energy, and a new group of investors had taken on the property), cocreator Pappy himself, who was a treasure trove of ideas, and MariRae and I as the coproducers of the program. MariRae directed the new episodes, and I directed the research and evaluation effort.

Not long after these initial meetings, we invited Dr. Ruth V. Small to head up the advisory board, not yet formed. Ruth brought expertise in the areas of instructional design and evaluation, motivation, and direct experience working with children in the classroom. She was a professor and director of the school media program at the School of Information Studies at Syracuse University and an excellent addition to the team. It was important to bring on this person during the front-end analysis as she could contribute to both the planning (e.g., identifying potential advisory board members) and audience motivational analysis.

As part of the front-end analysis, we reviewed and critiqued all of the twenty-six existing episodes, identifying strengths and weaknesses, looked at other art-related television programs, talked to parents and children, and randomly sampled the mail from parents and kids that the initial programs had generated, looking for feedback and audience reaction. Naturally we combed the literature on child development, research in children's television, art and drawing, and motivation looking for other clues that would help inform our program planning effort for our audience of primarily five- to eight-year-olds.

The educational planning and motivational audience analysis were carried out in tandem, together representing the front-end analysis. We knew that there were educational flaws in the way that the drawing segments were handled, as well as the life skills themes, and we will briefly address some of those concerns when we discuss the new program objectives. However, because the prime focus of this book is the motivational design of children's media, I will concentrate on motivational audience analysis in the next several paragraphs.

As you may recall from chapter 3, the audience motivational analysis is where you describe your target audience's incoming motivational profile with respect to the four components of the ARCS model: attention, relevance, confidence, and satisfaction. Based on input from a variety of sources, described previously, we made educated guesses as to children's motivational entry level in each of these categories.

Attention

Based on what we know about attention research and children's media, as well as the existing *Pappyland* episodes, we felt the audience would not be highly attentive or interested in some aspects of the existing program. Children expect sophisticated media design and high-quality graphics, animated effects, and audio enhancements, or they will simply turn to another channel. We also felt that there was not enough in the original programs to adequately stimulate or spark children's interest in utilizing their own creative approaches; the mail we examined supported this assertion, as the children's submissions demonstrated that they mostly copied Pappy's drawings without adding their own originality or elaborating on the drawings from the televised episodes (this was also a flaw from an instructional design perspective, since addressing creativity entails opportunities for elaboration, and original thought). Attention would be a critical motivational goal, probably requiring numerous strategies to both gain and sustain attention.

Relevance

By now, you are aware that to achieve relevance, you must connect with what is important, relevant, or meaningful in the child's life. This will contribute to the program's "value." Children love art projects, so the drawing and coloring segments were highly relevant to most children. Relevance is diminished when content is presented that is beyond the abilities of the target audience. Our analysis showed that several of the drawings were too complex for children in the target audience, which would need to be addressed in future episodes. We also felt that the audience would find the program more relevant if producers paid attention to the kinds of drawings children say they want. This would help address the "familiarity" aspect of relevance. Overall, we felt that relevance was probably higher than attention and would be an important goal, but one that didn't require as many strategies as attention.

Confidence

While attention and relevance contribute to value, confidence (and satisfaction) contributes to expectation for success. We predicted that confidence could be variable across the audience spectrum, based on developmental level, individual differences in artistic ability, and previous experiences. We received feedback from parents that more time was needed on some of the drawings; adequate time is critical to the confidence component. For these reasons, building confidence would also become a crucial goal, requiring a concentrated effort.

Satisfaction

Satisfaction goes hand in hand with confidence. Satisfaction is related to extrinsic and intrinsic motivators. Recognition is a powerful extrinsic motivator. Verbalizing statements that support the intrinsic joy of drawing and coloring are intrinsic motivators. The existing programs gave little in the way of either. We also realized that if we were to include recognition as a strategy for extrinsic motivation using television as the medium, we would need to be concerned with another important aspect of satisfaction—equity. Since television is a mass medium, the question was, how do you achieve equity? Satisfaction would be an important goal but probably would not require as many strategies as either attention or confidence.

In addition to the educational issues, our analysis identified a number of production quality concerns, including program pacing, need for production elements that would enhance appeal, and an overall face-lift. Despite its shortcomings, the program had a loyal following in the limited number of markets in which it aired (more than 12,000 letters and drawings had been sent to Pappy at that point), and we were careful not to lose sight of the elements of the program that endeared it to its audience. Among those elements were Pappy's charisma, the interactive drawing and coloring segments in which children drew and colored along with Pappy, and the charm of the rustic setting and program support characters.

We knew that the ARCS model had been used in numerous applications, including multimedia, Web design, classroom-based learning, distance education, and so on. Our concern was that we were developing this program for a broadcast and cable market. Like most television productions, our project would have a demanding schedule. Individual episodes would have to be completed in a timely fashion in order to meet the satellite feed dates to television stations. For that reason, we needed a model that was practical, as well as theory based and prescriptive. We found that the heuristic approach of the ARCS model was both practical and time saving for initially designing motivational goals and then continuously generating strategies in the demanding and often whirlwind world of broadcast (and cable).

THE ADVISORY BOARD

The integrated approach I recommend calls for assembling an advisory board early in the process. Do not wait until you have solidly committed to a program direction, investing much time and many dollars before you bring this valuable group into the picture; their recommendations would be of little value at this point. They may also resent you for it, quite possibly resigning from their posts. As already mentioned, we brought in an individual very early on who could help us formulate the advisory board and provide additional input during the front-end analysis. With broad goals identified, we were ready for input from the advisory board.

Who Should Be on an Advisory Board?

Look to Gerry Lesser's book for ideas on individuals who can make contributions to your educational effort. Not all projects will be able to afford as many advisers as *Sesame Street* or other CTW projects enjoyed. However, that does not mean you cannot do a stellar job with fewer individuals who contribute expertise across a number of critical areas of concern to your project. With only a modest budget available for advisers, research, and evaluation, we knew *Pappyland* could benefit from lessons learned from CTW.

The *Pappyland* advisory board consisted of ten members, with Dr. Ruth Small serving as chairperson. Other members of the advisory board contributed a broad range of experience to the project, including educational psychology, creativity research, teaching, art education, parenting, community education outreach, television communications, instructional design, and evaluation.

Initial Advisory Board Input

While the project staff had already identified a number of issues that the new programs should address, we felt it was important to also receive feedback on the existing programs from the advisory board members. They watched a number of existing *Pappyland* episodes. Some of their concerns in terms of content presentation included the following:

- Educational content was either weak or unsubstantiated, especially with regard to the presentation of life skills; scripts had been written without consultation with subject matter experts or instructional designers.

- Some of the drawings were too complex for the primary target audience.
- In many instances, insufficient time was allowed for children to complete their drawings with Pappy, which could be a source of frustration and anxiety.
- Several episodes included inadvertent stereotyping in the drawing and coloring segments (e.g., Pappy was drawing a cartoon with a little girl in it. He said, "Since this is a little girl, let's make her dress pink." Ouch!)
- There was a potential for stifling creativity rather than enhancing it due to the lack of clearly defined educational goals related to the creativity content of the program.
- There was a need for making more meaningful connections with the target audience's experiences and goals.
- There were no opportunities for children to share their results with other members of the audience.
- The program lacked diversity.
- The programs neglected audiences with special needs; none of the programs were close-captioned.

The previous concerns were strictly related to the program's educational and motivational needs. The advisory board also confirmed opinions held by Pappy, the executive producer, MariRae, and me about its technical quality. Even though the original programs had been produced and edited at a high-end production facility with state-of-the-art equipment, high-quality digital tape, and excellent lighting, the production was lacking in other respects. The advisory board confirmed our beliefs when it noted the following:

- Program pace overall was too slow while the drawing and coloring segments were too fast.
- The editing of program elements was too loose, resulting in uncomfortable pauses.
- Graphics did not have the degree of sophistication expected by media-savvy children.
- There was a lack of visual or motion effects.
- The delivery was often stilted, especially when puppets were involved.
- Puppets and puppeteering needed improvement.

Meetings/Work Sessions

In addition to board members, producers and other staff members attended the advisory board meetings in an ex-officio capacity. Sometimes other guests also participated. After updates and status reports, all would roll up their sleeves and begin the work session tackling the challenge set for that day. Results of the initial work sessions included confirmation and articulation of educational and motivational goals for curriculum design. Decisions on appropriate and relevant program topics for the first new series of episodes, called the 300 Series, were also made. Participation was not limited to these work sessions alone. Advisers contributed in other ways as well, which will be discussed under "Design."

One of the most important lessons learned from *Sesame Street* is that producers and researchers/advisers can work collaboratively in designing children's programming that is both educational and entertaining. That view was adopted by the entire *Pappyland* team. Producers (and other creative contributors) had agreed to share production insight and creativity with advisers, and advisers were sharing their perspectives and expertise with program executives and staff.

GOALS AND OBJECTIVES

One of the most important accomplishments of the advisory board working with program staff members was the clarification of program goals and objectives. In the initial discussions, many questions were raised and most were answered from several viewpoints. This laid the groundwork for establishing consensus on the goals and objectives that would move the project forward. We will first look at a sampling of the educational goals and then focus in more depth on the motivational goals and objectives.

Educational Goals

The influence of the CTW model can be found in the curriculum design of *Pappyland*. One overarching educational goal of the program was to enhance creativity. While many children's educational programs at that time offered excellent program content across a number of subject areas from science to math as well as life skills, few addressed creativity as a primary educational goal. *Pappyland* was designed to fill that void in a way that also promoted the development of self-esteem. But how do you translate this broad goal to specific objectives? First, you must operationally define creativity for purposes of program design. We all know that a creative person can look at problems in new and different ways, can generate a variety of solutions, enjoys challenges, and has a high sense of curiosity. *Pappyland* would be designed to provide a natural outlet for children's creativity but, even more importantly, to provide a unique opportunity to actually expand creative potential by addressing specific skills and motivations that relate to creativity. We decided to address the skills proposed by noted creativity theorist E. Paul Torrance and others, who proposed that creativity is exhibited by individuals who can generate not only original ideas but also many ideas, and ones which represent flexibility of thought. Additionally, creativity is exhibited when children can elaborate on existing ideas. Let's take a look at several examples of educational/curriculum objectives as they relate to creativity (the drawing and coloring segments) before moving on to examples of motivational goals.

Examples of Educational/Curriculum Objectives

1. The child can elaborate on his or her drawings (i.e., adding his or her ideas to Pappy's basic drawing (elaboration).
2. The child can generate a title for his or her drawing that goes beyond simple description (e.g., title includes adjective, suggests motion, feelings, humor, or other dynamic quality).
3. The child can generate many ideas, such as multiple uses for an ordinary object (fluency).
4. The child can generate alternative ideas represented visually, verbally, through creative writing and/or music (flexibility):
   a. Suggests a different way of accomplishing a task.
   b. Can make up a different end to a story or provide a different title to a drawing.
   c. Responds creatively to "What if . . ." scenarios.
   d. Knows that often there is more than just one correct way, answer, or solution to a problem.
5. The child can visually and/or verbally represent unique or unusual uses for an object, shape, or other (originality).

In addition to these, the program also articulated cognitive goals such as recall and comprehension of the life-skill themes of the program that are beyond the scope of this chapter. Keep in mind that I use the word "educational" and "curriculum" somewhat interchangeably. However, the curriculum is actually more long-range, representing what we hope to accomplish over the course of the series of programs. Each individual program will include one or more specific objectives targeting aspects of the curriculum goals and objectives.

Motivational Goals and Objectives

As you know, the development of motivational goals is an overlay to the instructional or educational goals, several of which were described previously.

Pop Quiz

Question: What drives the development of motivational goals and objectives?

Answer: The audience motivational analysis. (Very good! A little praise.) Motivational goals related to value (attention and relevance) included capturing children's attention at the beginning of the program, sustaining their attention throughout, and stimulating children's interest in drawing and creativity. While it would be overkill to examine every motivational goal for each ARCS component, our audience analysis indicated that a concentrated effort was required for building and maintaining confidence. With that in mind, let's use the motivational goals and objectives related to expectation for success (confidence and satisfaction) as our detailed examples.

Confidence Motivational Goal and Objectives

Broad level goal: Pappyland will build confidence in the child's own unique abilities and talents. This goal relates mostly to drawing and coloring, but it also includes life skills.

Specific confidence objectives: A number of specific confidence-related objectives relate to the broader goal.

The child:

1. Demonstrates a sense of personal competence in his or her perceived drawing abilities both in connection with the *Pappyland* program and when drawing independently.
2. Feels that his or her drawing skills are constantly improving.
3. Is willing to take on new challenges such as exploring ideas that are different or extend beyond what Pappy demonstrates (e.g., making purposeful changes to Pappy's drawing, experimenting with different colors, etc.).
4. Equates his or her own personal effort and ability to his or her final product.
5. Indicates confidence in his or her ability to communicate self-contrived ideas, make good decisions, and deal with stressful situations.
6. Appreciates the positives of diversity.
7. Conveys a positive self-concept verbally and nonverbally.

Also related to a positive expectation for success are satisfaction goals and objectives.

Satisfaction Motivational Goal and Objectives
Broad level goal: Pappyland will promote a sense of both intrinsic and extrinsic satisfaction and accomplishment.

Specific satisfaction objectives: A number of objectives were developed to address the broad satisfaction goal.

The child:
1. Willingly displays the outcome or product of his or her artistic efforts (extrinsic satisfaction).
2. Feels a sense of intrinsic enjoyment in learning and practicing drawing skills (e.g., as demonstrated by engaging in more drawing on his or her own).
3. Indicates positive attitudes about self-experiences in viewing the *Pappyland* episodes both in terms of the drawing and program life-skill themes.
4. Indicates the desire or intention to view more *Pappyland* episodes.
5. Feels a sense of equity about participating in *Pappyland* drawing invitations.

THE WRITER'S NOTEBOOK

One of my jobs as director of research and evaluation was putting together the writer's notebook, another CTW influence. The writer's notebook played a significant role in facilitating the design and production of the program. It contained:

- A detailed breakdown of the program goals and objectives (educational and motivational)
- Suggestions of motivational strategies that would address each objective
- Examples of what the strategies might look like

In addition to contributing their expertise during the work sessions, members of the advisory board submitted sample treatments for program episodes that were submitted to the program executives and to MariRae and me as producers. A treatment tackled a theme or topic related to one of the program goals and objectives. It provided essential information about the topic, as well as suggestions on how to integrate the topic into the episode. Once the treatments were refined in terms of the educational design, they were reviewed during a lively creative session between the executive producer, cocreator, and the producers and staff from Creative Media Solutions.

A successful collaboration takes time. Initially the creative team was apprehensive that the academic types would take the fun out of the show with their focus on educational soundness. Instead, they discovered that the advisory board often had creative ideas to support the program's educational and motivational content.

Finally, with the help of both advisers and the *Pappyland* research interns, I gathered support articles to accompany treatments. All the previously listed factors were essential ingredients in the writer's notebook.

DESIGN

Please review the integration concept map presented in chapter 4 on page 39. Feeding into the design phase are the motivational strategies on the ARCS side, and production research and actual test production on the CTW side. This book is mostly concerned with designing motivational strategies, but to place them in their proper context, we must briefly consider the production elements. Let's start with motivational strategies, as they must be designed prior to scripting and other production-oriented tasks associated with the design phase.

Motivational Strategy Design

The motivational audience analysis informed our identification of motivational goals and objectives. Now, those goals and objectives would be revisited in order to determine possible motivational strategies to support each of them. The first task was brainstorming strategies, then prioritizing them, and finally sequencing them throughout a typical program. To illustrate, here are some of the actual strategies we used to achieve confidence-related objectives:

- Use encouraging statements at the beginning of the drawing segment, such as "You can do it!"
- Applaud the child's effort during the drawing activity.
- Create an atmosphere of artistic freedom (e.g., encourage viewers to choose their own colors, to be different if they want, to use their imag-

inations, and to explore other ways to express themselves even after the show has aired).
- Show different ways of tackling a drawing or show other examples, in addition to Pappy's way. If no examples are shown visually, discuss the possibilities before drawing.
- Have Pappy occasionally model nontraditional choices.
- Have other characters draw along once in a while. Elmer (Pappy's crotchety cabin mate, a crusty ole puppet character, but lovable in spite of himself) might be a good character to epitomize "artistic freedom" as he deviates widely from what Pappy draws. Make the point that art is a very individual thing.
- Tie effort to results. For example, let the child know that, if she practices, she will get better and better at drawing.
- Use familiar symbols and letters, moving gradually to the more abstract during the drawing segment (moving from the familiar to the less familiar is also a relevance strategy).
- Provide adequate time to complete a drawing or coloring segment.
- Encourage diversity in both the enactment of program themes and the drawing segments.
- Avoid assumptions such as "I'm sure it's that way for you!" in reference to preferences for color over no color. A better statement would be "I really like colors. How about you?"
- Avoid choosing colors that might appear stereotypical such as always putting a girl figure in dresses or using only pastels to colorize.
- Occasionally have Pappy make a mistake and then try to correct it. If a child's confidence is slipping because of the difficulty level of the drawing, then showing that no one is perfect is heartening.
- Let the child know that it's okay to ask for help with his or her drawing. A brother, sister, friend, or parent might help with the drawing while the younger child feels more comfortable with the coloring.

Here are some of the strategies used for the satisfaction component based on specific objectives.

- Have Pappy listen for the kids' ideas.
- Tell the viewer that his or her drawing is "special because you are the artist."
- Verbally reinforce the child's intrinsic pride in accomplishing his work.
- Acknowledge the child's special effort in making the picture come alive.

- Provide a showcase for viewer art.
- Make certain the system for showing viewer art is perceived by children as a fair one.
- At the end of the program, encourage the child to show his or her drawing to someone.
- Encourage the child to make up a story about his or her drawing as an after-viewing activity.
- Use more nontraditional names in greeting.
- Include more female characters and ethnicity.
- Consider a do-a-doodle segment that encourages a child to use his or her imagination.

Production Research/Production Testing

Tasks included preproduction research, production design, set design and construction, puppet design and construction, composing, arranging, and recording music for each episode (contracted to a separate recording studio), auditioning talent and puppeteers, and scripting from the first to final drafts. It is during the scripting process when the writer adds her magic that suggested motivational strategies would be embedded. Advisers were available if questions arose at any time during scripting. Every script was reviewed first by the director of research and evaluation (me), then submitted to one (and usually two) advisers for feedback, and then to the executive producer and cocreator along with each reviewer's comments. Once the final draft was approved, it was passed into the anxiously waiting hands of the production team who then tackled the script from a production point of view.

This aspect of the design phase also included breaking down final scripts for studio taping, mostly accomplished by the director with input from the script supervisor. Creative Media Solutions (CMS) had its own editing facilities, but not a studio. Thus arrangements to tape the episodes at a PBS affiliate had to be made. It was necessary to carefully coordinate with the station management and studio crew at the affiliate and our own CMS personnel. Our own personnel included the producers, director, script supervisor, animator, and production interns. Since miniature sets were involved, it was important for the studio to include excellent "ultimatte" capabilities (the ability to shoot live action in front of a blue screen and key miniatures in the background).

Our production budget did not afford us the opportunity to produce whole shows for the purpose of preproduction testing, as suggested by the

CTW model. However, we did test some of the program elements, especially the animated effects.

PRODUCTION/DEVELOPMENT

In this stage, if you've done your homework, it all comes together smoothly. But remember Murphy's Law and expect the unexpected. Being well prepared, however, helps avert avoidable disasters and saves money in production. Studio production is very costly, so do not leave decisions that should be made during the design (preproduction) phase until you get into the studio!

One of the most successful segments we added to the new series was the inclusion of a Hall of Frames. This segment addressed the intrinsic reward strategy (satisfaction component) suggested by providing children with an outlet for participation and recognition. Pappy would "pop" into the animated environment, a children's museum of their own art. This was the Hall of Frames, and Pappy was surrounded by pictures hanging on every virtual wall, cherished renderings sent in by viewers in response to the drawing and coloring segments. Each picture was specially framed (digitally) and appeared to be a showpiece. As lively music was played under, thirty to forty pictures would be featured in each new episode. We received thousands and thousands of pictures, however, and eventually we needed expanded opportunities for recognition. One way we accomplished this was by compressing the closing credits to roll along one side of the screen in order to showcase additional pictures sent in by children on the opposite side. Still, this was not enough, as we had anticipated, and a new avenue had to be opened to provide children with a sense of equity with respect to displaying their treasured creations. This avenue was the World Wide Web. Children's pictures were featured in a Web version of the Hall of Frames and rotated frequently in order to give as many children as possible a chance at seeing their own picture. Pappy would inform children in the television program that they could also visit the website to see more drawings sent in to *Pappyland*.

The program development included more elements to stimulate attention, such as quick transitions, audio effects, enhanced visual effects, and faster-paced editing. Still, the show enjoyed a mellow pace in comparison with some of its frenzied television counterparts. This was part of the program's charm that we felt needed to be preserved.

We produced one series each season consisting of thirteen new episodes, beginning with the 300 Series. Once we completed it, we used the results of its evaluation to inform production decisions for the the 400 Series. In this way, although we couldn't afford preproduction research or much formative research during actual production, we were still given the benefit of previous productions informing subsequent productions. Thus they served as our formative research. We also produced a 500 Series and 600 Series.

To accompany the episodes, we also produced a print-based learning and activity guide with suggestions for related program activities, suggested books to reinforce or expand the theme of the program, and episode drawings for the child to color and elaborate on.

EVALUATION

Evaluation is the final step in our integrated concept map. Implementation or the airing of programs in this case study is assumed, with the results of implementation feeding back to the evaluation component. Summative evaluation, generally conducted after a project is complete, is usually performed by an outside organization; this is to avoid any possibility that the results could be unintentionally biased by internal staff who want the program to succeed. Formative evaluation is often conducted in-house, as CTW has traditionally done. That was the case with *Pappyland*, as well. This is because the purpose of formative evaluation is to inform production decisions. However, since each evaluation came after its respective series production end date, it served as both summative evaluation for that series and formative evaluation for the next series. That is, the results would help to guide programming decisions for each subsequent series. For this reason, Ruth Small (chair of advisory board) and I would often design the methodology for the studies and the research questions we wanted answered but outsource the conduct of the study to university graduate students with research experience.

Formative evaluation is an important topic that is addressed more fully with respect to this case study in chapter 13.

FINAL NOTE

This chapter's discussion was limited to the production and redesign of the program itself. It should be noted that there was also a simultaneous marketing effort underway, for example, to identify potential merchandising

RESCUE EFFORTS

opportunities, sell video rights, and so on. Those were separate concerns of the overall project and ones in which neither I nor Creative Media Solutions was involved.

COMING UP NEXT...

Formative research/evaluation can be used to determine not only what educational strategies are working (or not) but also which motivational strategies are most effective. Formative research is the subject of chapter 12.

PRODUCER'S CHECKLIST

- ❏ *Pappyland* was a children's program designed for five- to eight-year-olds to stimulate interest in drawing and foster creativity.
- ❏ A front-end analysis of the program involved reviewing and critiquing the first twenty-six episodes to identify strengths and weaknesses, interview parents and children, sample mail sent in by children, and review the literature across several domains of knowledge.
- ❏ The program used the integrated approach suggested in chapter 4, combining the CTW and ARCS models.
- ❏ The *Pappyland* advisory board consisted of ten members with expertise across a number of disciplines related to program success in achieving its educational and motivational objectives.
- ❏ The creative staff and advisory board worked together in addressing and solving program issues.
- ❏ Program goals and objectives were developed that addressed curriculum content and motivation.
- ❏ A writer's notebook was developed that included detailed descriptions of goals and objectives, suggested strategies and examples, and offered sample program treatments. It also included articles related to program topics and themes.
- ❏ The design effort covered motivational strategies and addressed production-related issues, including script development.
- ❏ Production/development featured a new segment called Hall of Frames, which addressed the motivational objective of providing extrinsic motivation through recognition.
- ❏ Evaluation included both summative (after the fact) and formative (during production) research.

DIGGING DEEPER

Amabile, Teresa M. 1984. "Children's Artistic Creativity: Effects of Choice in Task Materials." *Personality and Social Psychology Bulletin* 10: 209–15.
———. 1982. "Children's Artistic Creativity: Detrimental Effects of Competition in a Field Setting." *Personality and Social Psychology* 45, no. 2: 357–76.
Arnone, Marilyn P. 1996. "Pappyland: Filling a Void in Educational Children's Television Programming." Internal document. Creative Media Solutions, Syracuse, N.Y.
Keller, J. M., and Keller, B. H. 1989. *Motivational Delivery Checklist*. Florida State University.
Torrance, E. P. 1972. *The Search for Satori*. Buffalo, N.Y.: Creative Education Foundation.
Torrance, E. P., and Goff, K. 1989. "A Quiet Revolution." *Journal of Creative Behavior* 23, no. 2: 136–45.

⑫

THE ROLE OF FORMATIVE EVALUATION

Formative research and evaluation were used to gather both qualitative and quantitative information throughout the production of *Pappyland* episodes. As noted in the previous chapter, we gathered most of our data after each series of episodes was complete. This could technically be considered summative evaluation because it was conducted at the end of each series, but we considered it formative evaluation as it informed production decisions related to the next production period.

REVELATIONS

While *Pappyland* placed an equal focus on life skills and creative self-expression in the first new series, the 300 Series, the 400 and 500 Series placed a stronger emphasis on creativity. How did *Pappyland* evolve to this point? In addition to collecting anecdotal data and feedback from numerous sources, the formative research for the 300 Series told us that the golden nuggets of the program were the art-related segments—the opportunities for children to express themselves. This can be seen from the following quotations taken from a report on formative research conducted in Los Angeles, California: "Almost all students, regardless of grade level, were exceptionally focused during both the drawing and coloring segments. Their work seemed to be very important to them" (Arnone and Small 1998, 11).

"At the end of the drawing, the picture came to life and this was a definite attention-grabber, probably because it also contained music and sound effects. However, immediately following the animation, a number of children went back to drawing as Pappy walked from his drawing table to the character(s) to engage in a dialog pertaining to the program theme. Here is where attention momentarily waned. The drawing segment was officially concluded but many children were so committed to finishing their drawings that they appeared not to be listening to the dialog" (Arnone and Small 1998, 13).

As this quote indicates, some children wanted to continue working on their drawings after the segment had concluded. The production team responded by modifying the program design, placing a segment after the drawing that allowed the viewer time to keep working on his or her drawing without losing out on the overall storyline of the program. Pappy told viewers that it was okay to keep drawing or finish up later. One aspect of encouraging creativity on which experts agree is that open-ended time is important to fostering creativity. As you will recall from previous chapters, time is an important element related to confidence. You will increase a child's expectation for success if you provide adequate time to complete a task. Furthermore, encouraging children to finish up later, if they wish, increases the probability that they will enter a state of "flow" when they have fewer distractions (e.g., the television is turned off).

Although providing details about the methodology, data analysis, and interpretation for each set of formative evaluations is beyond the scope of this chapter, you need to have a sense of how we approached these tasks. With that in mind, I will describe one formative evaluation study (Los Angeles) and then briefly mention several other studies and methods that were undertaken to explore the educational viability and motivational soundness of the series.

THE LOS ANGELES STUDY

We were concerned that the program lacked diversity, and we wanted to see how it would fare in an urban environment with a large population of minorities. We chose two schools for participation, one of which was located in south central Los Angeles.

Study Participants

Eighty-seven children in kindergarten through third grade participated. Almost all the children represented minority groups, mostly African American (n = 29) and Hispanic (n = 47); the remainder were Caucasian, Asian, or Filipino. None of the children had been previously exposed to *Pappyland,* since it had begun airing only two months before. A small group of parents and educators also participated in the evaluation through a parent/focus group that was conducted at a suburban magnet school.

What Data We Collected and How

We collected data on attention, participation, general program appeal, comprehension of program themes, and issues such as the pace of the drawing and coloring segments. Consequently this evaluation would shed light on both educational and motivational issues. We also collected recommendations from children on the types of drawings they wanted to see in future programs. Several methods were used to gather both qualitative and quantitative data, including observation, questionnaires, and separate focus groups for children and parents/educators. We found that the observations and focus groups provided the most useful information.

Children in kindergarten through third grade watched a *Pappyland* episode and participated in the drawing and coloring segments as the researchers observed. All viewed the programs in their own classrooms. Attention to general and specific program elements and overt participation were the two primary categories of interest during the observations. Researchers were given an observation protocol to follow.

What We Found: Some Highlights

We found that the kindergarten children were attracted to the television set as soon as the upbeat *Pappyland* theme song began. This age-group, however, is easily distracted by any movement or physical activity, such as the teacher or aide crossing the room. While these distractions initially commanded precedence, they initially subsided, and children became more focused on the television set. This initial behavior was also noted with the first-grade students.

Observing children across the age range that the grades represented was extremely useful. It gave us a chance to see which segments resulted in the highest attention, which characters got the most smiles and verbalizations, and where attention waned, even momentarily. As already noted, the greatest attention was paid during the drawing and coloring segments, and yet it also served as an opportunity for some children to interact with one another. Some children, regardless of grade level, seemed to enjoy comparing their pictures and showing off their good drawings. Does this ring any bells with you in regard to something we discussed in chapter 3 and then again in chapter 6? Think back to McClelland's theory of achievement motivation. Perhaps these children were high in need for affiliation and the drawing and coloring segments were opportunities for them to share their drawings and socialize with other children. Others were, in contrast, very intent on completing their own drawings and did not seek feedback from their peers. Perhaps these were children high in need for achievement, preferring to work independently. *Pappyland,* viewed in a group situation, seemed to accommodate both these motives, and, as you will recall, motive matching is key to the relevance component of the ARCS model.

The elements of music, humor (the younger children especially liked Elmer's silly jokes), surprise, novelty, character appeal, and questioning (e.g., "What color do you think would work here?") were responsible for most overt actions such as smiling, verbalizations, laughter, and movement. A popular segment in terms of attention-sustaining ability was the Hall of Frames, where drawings that children had sent in were framed in an animated museumlike gallery. Children seemed very interested in artwork sent in by other children their age.

Children generally laughed at the different types of humor. Most children liked the visual humor (e.g., slapstick, as when Pappy drew a clown standing next to a ladder with a bucket of water on top; when the clown came to life and danced around, he accidentally kicked the leg of the ladder and the bucket of water fell on his head). Third-grade students could appreciate the verbal humor (e.g., Elmer's silly jokes) more than the younger students. This is consistent with what we know from the research on developmental differences in children's appreciation of verbal humor.

Although a large number of children in kindergarten through second grade actively responded (moving, tapping their feet, tapping their hands, etc.) to the musical aspects of the program including a songster named Sing-A-Song Sam, the third graders were less impressed with this aspect of the program. Several snickered when the song segment began and few paid attention to it, choosing instead to focus on their drawings.

Educational Content

Most children were able to recall the theme and educational content of the program viewed because it was reinforced several times. In the children's focus group, children were able to connect the overall program theme with the theme of the song featured in the episode. We had made certain that the writers understood the importance of clearly defining the concept or skill a program tackles and presenting the content in ways that the audience will comprehend. Suggestions we had provided prior to production included representing the content more than once and in more than one way (e.g., using alternate ways to represent a concept or skill: verbally through dialog, visually, reinforcement through drawing and animation, restatement, etc.).

About Diversity

While the children never overtly mentioned the lack of diversity, the parents in our focus group did. We received a great deal of excellent feedback from this session. Race, physical disability, and language disabilities were suggestions offered, as well as diversity in terms of what makes up a family. One parent commented, "There's no longer that typical father and mother. Mrs. Doubtfire [character in movie] has a strong message, that a grandma could be a family."

Since Pappy was Caucasian, and most of the support cast were animal puppets, we added diversity into future programs by incorporating more minorities in the drawings. Another way was to have special guest children visit *Pappyland* from time to time. One episode, for example, featured a hearing-impaired child.

Sharing Results with the Creative Team

The results of the formative research and evaluation studies were presented to the creative team in layman's terms with specific recommendations on how to incorporate what we learned into new episodes of the program. In addition to specific comments about *Pappyland* and our study, we sprinkled in some general ones drawn from the research in children's television. To give you an idea of how our information was presented, here are several of the recommendations to the creative staff as a result of the Los Angeles study (from Small, Arnone, Thompson, and Mehra 1996):

- Repetition can be thought of as expectancies. Children can look forward to Pappy entering the cabin and going through his regular routine, but research also shows that children will appreciate some variety within the repetition or routine. This is often accomplished in children's programs by varying the routine or the content while still maintaining some predictability. For example, once in a while Pappy might

have characters pop into the cabin during the opening or perhaps have a little more patter with Binky the Brush than he generally does. He could also forget to say hi to GrandPappy Pappy [a talking portrait of Pappy's grandpappy on the wall] and the "viewers" could remind him. Children find humor in adults making mistakes.
- Action is important.
  - Some research has indicated that children love action in the form of slapstick. This is not to say that the slapstick must have a harmful outcome in order to be appealing. Often it is the silly, nonsensical, unexpected, physically exaggerated and incongruous forms of slapstick that appeal most to children in the younger age group to primary grades.
  - Other kinds of action that could be used include maximizing the action potential of the Color Copter [a kind of helicopter Pappy uses to travel around Pappyland] which really appealed to children in this evaluation, and using action-oriented special effects or transitions. Sound also helps create a sense of action.
- Humor is important in children's programming. When it does not distract from the content or educational message, humor is a wonderful way of sustaining attention. Naturally slapstick is as much a part of humor as it is of action, but there are other ways of including humor. Children often love to engage in wordplay (not including wordplay that is derived from double meanings, or plays on words). *Pappyland* has several word plays or catch phrases that are used from time to time. These include "Pappyriffic!" and "There's no limitation to your imagination!" Catch phrases or words are associated with characters, for example. Elmer's catch phrase has become "Hey, Sonny . . . Don't you know what time it is?!" Some children in our sample picked right up on that and began mimicking Elmer.

Other recommendations included (briefly):

- Do more drawings of animals. Take the suggestions (we have a number of them) directly from our target audience. Include machines too, such as airplanes, trains, or maybe rockets that go into outer space. Show differences in drawings by different individuals (e.g., even a puppet character's drawing could help accomplish this). Balance the inclusion of boys and girls and of minorities in the drawings.
- Use "Color Copter" more often. Perhaps the Color Copter could be greeted in the opening segment occasionally and could respond by

revving its engine or spinning its propeller with an accompanying sound effect. Build this as a character and use in place of other portals more often [portals were ways that Pappy used to go from place to place such as through his sketch pad, or using a special door, etc.]. Perhaps the Color Copter could even be a featured player in an episode.
- Enhance the memorability factor of Sing-A-Song Sam. Give him more to say once in a while in order to build his "character" rather than just have him proceed immediately into a song.
- Vary the complexity of drawings. While pacing did not seem to be a big issue to the children in this study, the kindergarteners and first graders did lag behind in their drawings. This might also help in terms of attention loss after drawings as children attempt to finish their drawings.
- Emphasize the "manners" potential of Lily. Both parents and children liked that aspect of the character with parents referring to her as "gracious."
- Find ways of including more diversity in the program. When asked what he remembered most about Sing-A-Song Sam, one second grader in the focus group recalled, "He was white." Continue using racially diverse names when Pappy greets children at home. Children and parents loved that.
- Include more sound effects, musical stings, and music in general to sustain attention. Keep the pace and action of the show up by incorporating more visual impact such as animation and effects. Consider, for example, adding music or other pacing devices to spice up the coloring segment, which was perceived by some parents as too long and too slow.
- Regarding nonbroadcast support, include helpful guidelines for teachers who would like to incorporate *Pappyland* into their schedule. This would include tips that range from making the most of the drawing and coloring segments to including the song lyrics in the activity guides. This could also include a section in which a number of teachers describe ways in which they are integrating *Pappyland* into their classroom activities.

As you were reading these suggestions, were you placing them in ARCS categories? You can readily see how strong the motivational aspects of a program must be.

Caveat

Could we generalize from this one study about what would work in other markets? Of course not, and we made this clear in our report. Collecting data from other markets, we noted, would help us substantiate the findings from this study. From examining the data from this study, however, we were able to make predictions about what we might find in similar markets.

OTHER FORMATIVE RESEARCH AND EVALUATION EFFORTS

Our budget limited the amount of travel we could do in conjunction with our research efforts. Even so, we were able to collect useful information in similar studies in our own central New York area using observation, focus groups, and questionnaires. The difference was that *Pappyland* was a household word in this area as opposed to the obscurity it was afforded in the Los Angeles market. Since that study, we had made some modifications in the program, including the addition of several new characters; one was DoodleBug, a boisterous green bug who regularly challenged Pappy to doodle duels. Sometimes, at the end of the program, DoodleBug interrupted the credits and challenged the kids to create a drawing out of his doodle. This encouraged originality and became a popular segment. Our research in central New York confirmed some of the things we learned in Los Angeles and improved our awareness of other issues, as well.

We felt it was important to interview parents. Many shared good ideas that would help kids stretch their imaginations. Some parents suggested that viewers think of a story about the picture they just drew. We began incorporating this idea into the coloring segments. We also started using unconventional colors in the coloring segments as a result of feedback from parents and educators. For example, one parent said, "What about a purple tree with orange leaves?" Why not?

We constantly tried new things and then used our evaluations to determine how successful they were. We needed to know the extent to which the educational objectives specified in the educational guidelines had been accomplished, the impact of viewing *Pappyland* on children's attitudes toward drawing and self-expression, the program elements that were working (or not) and with whom, what children learn and enjoy, and always how the programs could be improved or enhanced.

One study explored the effect of our nonbroadcast print support material on children's recall and comprehension of central program content and on children's creativity in a coloring task.

We also conducted a small but multifaceted study exploring Web-related issues. It involved children interacting with the *Pappyland* website, comparisons with other websites, and a parent survey. The main research question in part 1 of this study was, how do children rate the *Pappyland* website on issues that relate to its impact on motivation? This study was challenging because it was difficult to determine whether some of the less positive reactions of children were due to the actual content of the website or their frustration with the time it took for media-rich materials to load, such as games and animations. Consider that this study was undertaken in 1998, when speed and access issues were still a major issue. What we learned from this study was to pay more attention to the lowest common denominator when using new technologies. Our researchers also conducted surveys with parents to garner their perceptions of their children's viewing of *Pappyland*. Finally, researchers explored other children's television websites and compared features with those offered on the *Pappyland* website.

One last study worth noting was conducted in San Antonio, Texas. This was also in 1998, when *Pappyland* had been airing in most markets on The Learning Channel. We needed a market that hadn't been exposed to *Pappyland* for this study. Fortunately, a section of northeast San Antonio was not yet set up for cable. A total of eighty-one subjects, primarily of Hispanic origin, in grades 1, 2, and 3 participated in this longitudinal study. The experimental group watched twenty-six episodes of the 500 and 600 Series in their classrooms twice a week from early February 1998 through mid-May of the same year. The program would be viewed three times in the week following school vacations. Because this section of town was not yet "cabled," none of the subjects had previous exposure to the *Pappyland* programs, which provided a unique opportunity to study the effects of viewing the program (over an extended period of time) on children's creativity and willingness to use their own personal style, as described in several of the program's objectives. Following the extended treatment (watching *Pappyland* versus not watching *Pappyland*), all students were exposed to a drawing and a coloring segment from the program that the experimental group (those who watched *Pappyland* regularly) had not yet seen. For the control group (those who had never seen *Pappyland*), this was the first time they were introduced to Pappy Drew-It. Children were to draw and color with Pappy and were instructed to add their own style and ideas. Strict protocols were used (e.g., an administrator script) in order to increase reliability across all administrations of the test. We looked at several aspects of creativity, including elaboration, fluency, and originality. The drawings were rated by three trained (in scoring) art educators, who eventually came to a 90 percent interrater consensus as a result of training. The three subscores on elaboration, fluency, and originality were combined for a total creativity score. There was a significant difference between the control group and the experimental group on all three scores and on the total creativity score. Factorial analyses were conducted to determine interaction effects and none could be found for either gender or grade. Time on task data was also collected. The experimental groups spent considerably more time completing their pictures than did the control groups. These results were heartening. Encouraging children to take their time when drawing and coloring paid off, as well as all the strategies we had embedded to build confidence and stretch the child's imagination. Again, this study took place in San Antonio and we could not make any generalizations based on the results. We would have to replicate these results many times before we could do that.

However, the results of all the formative research and evaluations were crucial for our own in-house purposes. Those purposes were to continually fine-tune our program's goals and objectives, and guide new program ideas to nurture creativity and stimulate children's intrinsic motivation to draw.

FINAL NOTE

Pappyland was targeted at five- to eight-year-old children, and most of our formative evaluations involved children in this age-group. However, we know that the program also appealed to a broader age range, both younger and older. This fact was supported by the enormous number of letters and drawings received each week from the audience. It seems that some of the younger viewers (under 5) watched with older siblings or parents. We always included drawings sent in by these younger viewers in both the Hall of Frames segments and the closing credits, as well as on the *Pappyland* website's Hall of Frames counterpart. Likewise, we received mail from much older viewers and even some adults. Many older viewers indicated that drawing along with Pappy helped them gain confidence in drawing skills they previously felt they lacked.

COMING UP NEXT ...

You will find a few concluding thoughts in chapter 13. They include how you might use this book as a handy reference when you tackle your next (or first) children's media project.

DIGGING DEEPER

Arnone, Marilyn, and Small, Ruth. 1998. "Formative Evaluation Summary Report: Pappyland: 500/600 Television Series." Internal Document, Creative Media Solutions, Syracuse, N.Y.

Small, Ruth, Arnone, Marilyn, Thompson, Wendy, Mehra, Jhilmil. 1996. "Pappyland Formative Evaluation Report: Central New York." Internal Document, Creative Media Solutions, Syracuse, N.Y.

Small, Ruth, Arnone, Marilyn, Thompson, Wendy, Mehra, Jhilmil, Alpern, Jules, and Disiki, Audra. 1996. "Formative Evaluation Report: Los Angeles Study." Internal Document, Creative Media Solutions, Syracuse, N.Y.

Small, Ruth V., Meyer, Jennifer, and Scheer, Abby Kasowitz. 1997. "Formative Evaluation Report: Central New York." Internal Document, Creative Media Solutions, Syracuse, N.Y.

⓭

A FEW CLOSING THOUGHTS

Pappyland provided me with excellent material for a case study. As I think back on it, the program was ideal for incorporating the types of motivational goals and strategies suggested by the ARCS model. At the time there were several programs which taught art/drawing from a technical perspective. That was not the primary aim of *Pappyland*. More than a drawing show, it provided opportunities for children to discover their own talents, challenged them to think of original ideas, and posed questions designed to stretch their imaginations. While all of these strategies nurture creativity, they were likewise motivational.

Art is an ideal medium to build self-esteem, which can also be related to confidence. Children who participated in the program were building confidence in their budding abilities and were producing results (artwork) they could be proud of. While we didn't have a budget to follow up with regular viewers, we were hoping that their successes might transfer to other areas of life. Successful experiences in one area can help set the stage for successes in other areas.

When they were provided further opportunities for recognition of their accomplishments in both the television program and its Web counterpart, the satisfaction component of the ARCS model kicked in. Yet extrinsic satisfaction was not the only desired objective in terms of satisfaction; we also wanted viewers to realize intrinsic satisfaction with their drawing. To this end, Pappy would remind children to think of how drawing and coloring made them feel inside. He helped children understand that the rewards of drawing and coloring were simply drawing and coloring.

The program attempted to select topics relevant to the child's experience and developmental level, and the new series began tackling drawing segments that children themselves had suggested, such as their favorite animals, machines, even space. These changes increased the perceived "relevance" of the program by its target audience. Finally, by adding new elements and special effects to the program, *Pappyland* was able to gain and sustain attention without losing the charm of its easygoing pace. Remember, its unhurried pace was identified as part of its uniqueness as a television offering for children, proving what *TV Guide* writer Moira McCormick aptly affirmed "challenged the belief that kids have nanosecond attention spans."

One of the greatest strengths of the program with its art-based content was that it encouraged interactivity or active participation. Research has shown that active participation is one of the best ways of learning. Active participation is also a motivator that helps sustain attention at a high level. By the way, a new program for older children featuring Pappy and art is currently in the works and promises to be an interactive application converging television and the Internet.

As you consider your first or next children's media project, whether that project is television, video, print, Web-based, or even a software application, I strongly urge you to consider an integrative approach to development that brings in the strengths of a CTW model and incorporates the necessary focus on motivation that a successful project demands. For that aspect of your design, the ARCS model provides a solid framework grounded in motivation theory but is also prescriptive. Most of us do not have time to get too absorbed in theory, and the practical value of the model is what makes it ideal for applying to the design of children's media.

A FINAL NOTE

I recommend using chapter 4 as a quick reference or guide to the overall development effort; check back on chapters 5–8 (motivational strategies) whenever you want to spark an idea for your own project or when you find yourself working on one that could use a motivational makeover.

Producing children's media that inform and entertain is a rewarding enterprise (motivationally speaking, of course). My wish for you is that you will experience both the intrinsic and extrinsic satisfaction that comes with the job of children's media producer.

Appendix A

WEBMAC FOR CHILDREN'S TV WEBSITES

WebMAC for Children's TV Websites

Copyright 2004, Marilyn P. Arnone and Ruth V. Small

NAME: _____   AGE: _____

GRADE: _____   DATE: _____

TV WEBSITE VISITED: _____

INSTRUCTIONS

Just like the judges who decide the winners in an art or science contest, you are one of the judges for this website. As someone who watches the television show, we thought you would be a good judge of its website! After reading each question, circle the face that best describes how you would rate this website. Remember that there are no right or wrong answers. First, try the example below.

EXAMPLE

Did this website include things that you are interested in?

☹   😐   🙂   😃
0   1   2   3

If you circle the *sad face* ☹, it means that this website is **really poor** in this category. In other words, there is nothing in this website that is of interest to you. You give it the lowest score, which is 0 points. If you circle the face with *no expression* 😐 (just a straight line for the mouth), it means that this website is **O.K. but there's nothing special** that interests you so you give it 1 point. If you circle the face with a *small smile*, it means that this website is not the best but it is **good** which is 2 points. If you circle the face with a *big smile* 😃, it means that this website is **excellent** – definitely one of the best websites you have seen when it comes to things that interest you. You give it 3 points, the highest score.

APPENDIX A

WebMAC for Children's TV Websites — page 1

1. How well does the home page get your attention?

   0   1   2   3

2. How well can you read and understand the words that are used?

   0   1   2   3

3. How well does this website create the look and feel of the TV show?

   0   1   2   3

4. How easy is it to find your way around this website without getting lost?

   0   1   2   3

5. Are there enough choices for things to do at this website?

   0   1   2   3

6. How well do all of the parts of this website work?

   0   1   2   3

7. Are all your favorite characters from the TV show at this website?

   0   1   2   3

8. How quickly do things like pictures, games, or videos come up on the screen?

   0   1   2   3

9. How much do you feel like participating in the activities at this website?

   0   1   2   3

WebMAC for Children's TV Websites — page 2

10. How well do the games and activities match your age level?

    0   1   2   3

11. How well do you think other children your age will like visiting this website?

    0   1   2   3

12. Is it easy to get help if you need it at this website?

    0   1   2   3

13. Does this website make you feel curious about learning new things?

    0   1   2   3

14. How confident are you that you can do the activities at this website?

    0   1   2   3

15. Are you learning new things that you didn't learn from the TV show?

    0   1   2   3

16. When you click on something, how quickly do you get what you want?

    0   1   2   3

17. Are there ways of sharing your own work or ideas at this website?

    0   1   2   3

18. How simple and clear are the directions for using this website?

    0   1   2   3

APPENDIX A

WebMAC for Children's TV Websites — page 3

19. How do you rate this website compared to other TV show websites you've seen?

    ☹ 0   😐 1   🙂 2   😊 3

20. How easy is it to find what you are looking for at this website?

    ☹ 0   😐 1   🙂 2   😊 3

21. Does this website include enough new things to do or learn about?

    ☹ 0   😐 1   🙂 2   😊 3

22. Does this website give you enough control of where you go and what you do?

    ☹ 0   😐 1   🙂 2   😊 3

23. How often do you think this website has new things to do or learn about?

    ☹ 0   😐 1   🙂 2   😊 3

24. Does this website tell you how well you are doing in the activities?

    ☹ 0   😐 1   🙂 2   😊 3

25. How much can you use what you learn at this website at home or at school?

    ☹ 0   😐 1   🙂 2   😊 3

26. How confident are you to try new games or activities at this website?

    ☹ 0   😐 1   🙂 2   😊 3

One more page and you are done! ➡

WebMAC for Children's TV Websites — page 4

27. Is this website as much fun as or more fun than its TV show?

    ☹ 0   😐 1   🙂 2   😃 3

28. Is it easy to contact someone at the website if you have a question or problem?

    ☹ 0   😐 1   🙂 2   😃 3

29. How well do the pictures, animations, sounds, or videos hold your attention?

    ☹ 0   😐 1   🙂 2   😃 3

30. Does this website provide the right amount of challenge for you?

    ☹ 0   😐 1   🙂 2   😃 3

31. How much do you trust the factual information on this website?

    ☹ 0   😐 1   🙂 2   😃 3

32. How good a job does this website do in telling kids about their privacy rights?

    ☹ 0   😐 1   🙂 2   😃 3

⟹ What do you like best about this website? Write in the space below.

⟹ What would make this website better? Write your ideas below.

Appendix B

WEBMAC FOR CHILDREN'S TV WEBSITES

Administrator Directions, Scoring Guidelines, Score Sheets, and Grids

The length of the WebMAC for Children's TV Websites activity demands more time than is available in a one-period classroom situation with a large group of children. It works well in a facilitated focus group and in one-on-one interview situations with children between eight and eleven years. It can be adapted for younger or older children, and may also be adapted for online administration. Depending on your purpose, situation, or resources, you can have children complete the evaluation independently or as small groups.

ADMINISTRATION DIRECTIONS

1. Make sure that children understand common terms used in discussing websites. For example, a homepage is the starting place. Here you can find out what is on the website. A link is a way of connecting to another source of information. A button is what you click in order to move from one place to another within a website or to link to another website. Every children's website has a privacy policy to protect children's privacy rights, and so on.
2. Briefly discuss the television program and collect some preliminary information such as how many are regular viewers, viewing frequency,

age, and so on. This information may be useful later as you analyze the results of the evaluation.
3. Have each child or small group peruse the website and interact with it for a predetermined length of time (e.g., 15–25 minutes). Allow adequate time for your particular site.
4. Provide each child or small group with the WebMAC evaluation instrument.
5. Read the instrument directions aloud including the example item on the cover page. Each child should clearly understand that WebMAC for Children's TV websites is not a test but rather a way for them to give important feedback to the producers and designers of the website. If working with children who have low reading ability, you may need to read each question aloud.
6. Having younger children use rulers to keep their place may also help. You could then say, "Put your ruler under the faces for question 1. Listen carefully. [Read question.] Think about your experience with this website. Then circle the face that represents how you feel."

SCORING

Scores range from 0 to 3 for each item.

Using the reproducible scoring sheet provided on the next page, add up all the odd-numbered items under column A and all the even-numbered items under column B for each child. If this instrument is given in conjunction with a focus group, a general discussion could ensue relating to specific questions for which you desire additional qualitative feedback. A focus group should be recorded and later transcribed for analysis.

You can quickly summarize the data using the group tally form included with these directions.

For a visual representation of results, plot the average scores on the grid provided.

INDIVIDUAL SCORING SHEET

Place the score for each question next to the number of that question. Notice that odd-numbered questions are under column A and even-numbered questions are under column B.

A	B
1. _____	2. _____
3. _____	4. _____
5. _____	6. _____
7. _____	8. _____
9. _____	10. _____
11. _____	12. _____
13. _____	14. _____
15. _____	16. _____
17. _____	18. _____
19. _____	20. _____
21. _____	22. _____
23. _____	24. _____
25. _____	26. _____
27. _____	28. _____
29. _____	30. _____
31. _____	32. _____
Total A: _____	Total B: _____

GROUP TALLY SHEET: SUMMARIZING THE RESULTS

Use the group tally sheet in this section to record each child's total scores for A and B. Add up the scores where indicated. Then average each list and plot the overall average scores on the grid on the next page.

Individual Total A Scores	Individual Total B Scores
1. _____	1. _____
2. _____	2. _____
3. _____	3. _____
4. _____	4. _____
5. _____	5. _____
6. _____	6. _____
7. _____	7. _____
8. _____	8. _____
9. _____	9. _____
10. _____	10. _____
11. _____	11. _____

12. _____	12. _____
13. _____	13. _____
14. _____	14. _____
15. _____	15. _____
16. _____	16. _____
17. _____	17. _____
18. _____	18. _____
19. _____	19. _____
20. _____	20. _____
Total A Scores: _____	Total B Scores: _____
Average A Scores: _____	Average B Scores: _____

INTERPRETATION

The "A" score reflects the summary motivation score on the value dimension. It shows how interesting and relevant or meaningful this website is to the child. It also encompasses attributes of the website that gain and sustain attention. A low score indicates that this child evaluator feels the site lacks value for him or her. The "B" score reflects the summary motivation score on the expectation for success (XS) dimension. This covers things like how easy or difficult it was to find his or her way around, how well the site elements worked, how clear the information was, and how satisfying the experience was. A low score here indicates, for example, that the child did not feel confident or satisfied that he or she could easily navigate or get the desired information. Thus the child has a low expectation for success in this website environment. Following is the score key:

A Score (Value)

0–12 Poor
13–23 Below Average
24–32 Average/Above Average
33–40 Good
41–48 Outstanding

B Score (Expectation for Success)

0–12 Poor
13–23 Below Average
24–32 Average/Above Average
33–40 Good
41–48 Outstanding

VISUALIZING THE SCORES

Figure 6 is a grid reference that you can use to help visualize the results of each child's evaluation and/or plot the summary scores of all children's evaluation results. On the grid, you will notice that the horizontal line is for the Value score (the "A" score) and the vertical line is for the Expectation for Success (XS) score (the "B" score). As you can see, the upper right quadrant is most desirable, representing average to high scores for both value and expectation for success while the lower left quadrant represents the least desirable scores. (An awesome website will have scores in the extreme upper right quadrant.) See the next section for an example of plotting scores.

EXAMPLE OF PLOTTING SCORES

Figure 7 is an example of plotting scores for a fictitious website. In this case, the Value score is 40 and the Expectation for Success (XS) score is 18. Their intersection point falls within the lower right quadrant of the grid. This indicates that in this child's opinion, this television program–related website is interesting and has a good value; but due to certain factors that may include functionality problems with the website, this child's expectation for success (which includes confidence and satisfaction

High Expectation for Success

Awsome Web Site!

Average to high for expectation for success/Below average to low for value

Average to high for value/Average to high for expectation for success

Low Value 0 ———————24———————48 **High Value**

Below average to low for value/Below average to low for expectation for success

Average to high for value/Below average to low for expectation for success

Low Expectation for Success

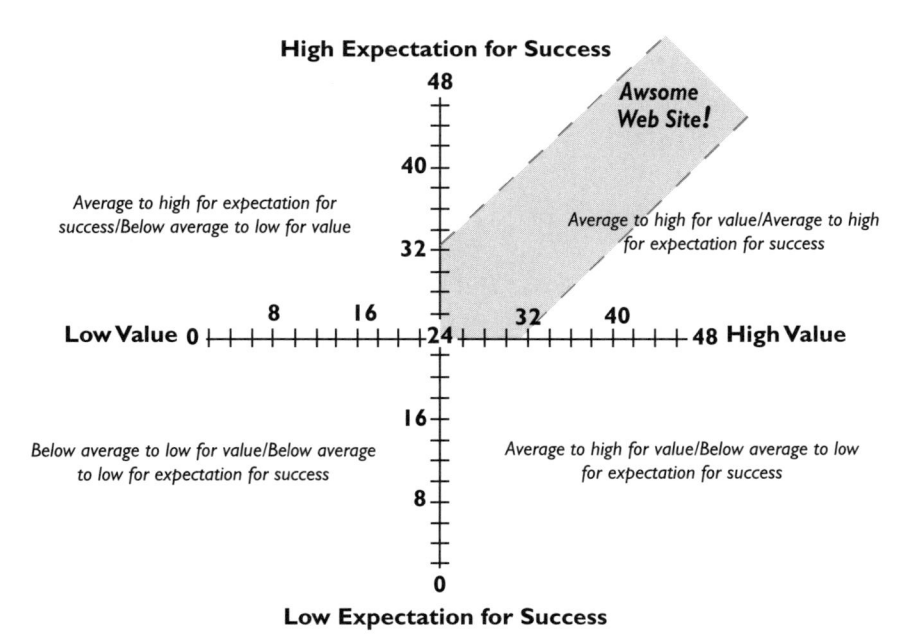

Figure 6.   Grid reference

High Expectation for Success

```
                    48
                    +
                    40
                    +
                    32
         8    16    +    32    40
Low Value 0 ├──────┼──24──────○──── 48 High Value
                    ○ ·············· X 40V;18XS
                    16
                    +
                    8
                    +
                    0
```

Low Expectation for Success

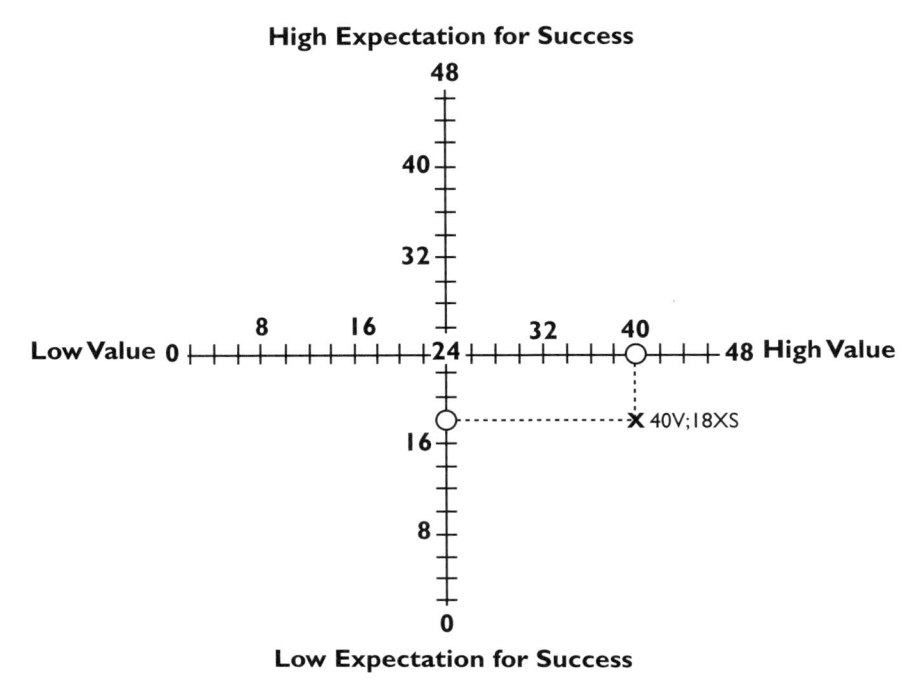

Figure 7. Plotting scores for a fictitious website

factors) is below average. Use the blank grid on the next page as a template for plotting results of either individual children's scores or summary scores.

BLANK TEMPLATE FOR PLOTTING SCORES

The reproducible grid in figure 8 can be used to record either individual scores or summary scores for a group of children. To record the actual scores on the scoring grid:

1. Plot the score for V along the Value continuum and the score for XS along the Expectation for Success continuum.
2. Draw straight lines to the intersection point.
3. Check the reference grid to explain results.

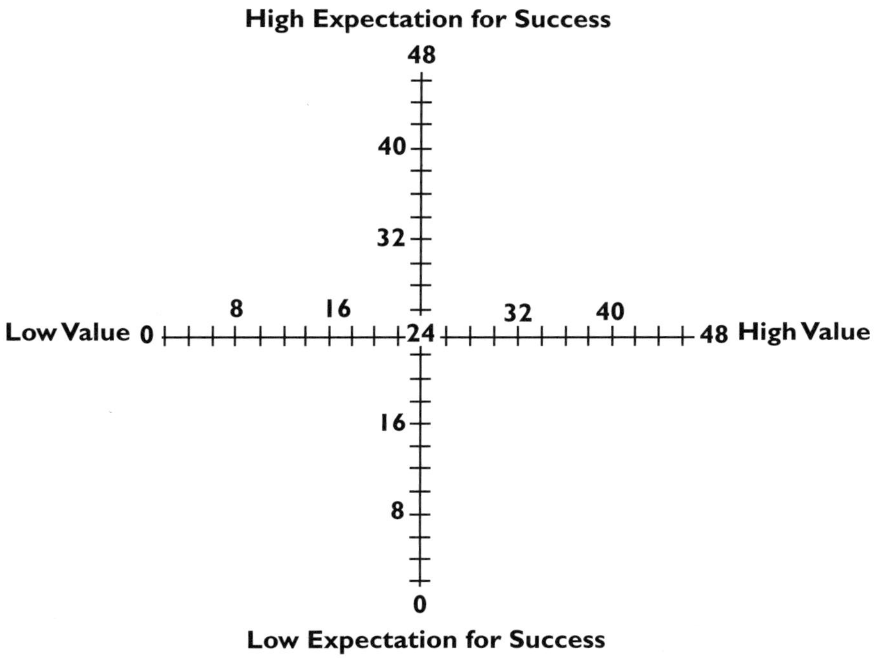
High Expectation for Success
48
40
32
8
16
Low Value 0
24
32
40
48 High Value
16
8
0
Low Expectation for Success

Figure 8. Blank template for plotting scores

INDEX

ability, 25; attribution to, 24, 26, 76, 77–79, 83, 86, 87, 91
accessible web design, 107–9
achievement motivation theory, 67. *See also* goal orientation; McClelland, David; motive matching
achievement, 24, 33, 64, 85, 96, 100, 101; need for, 25, 67, 68, 73, 146
ADA. *See* Americans with Disabilities Act
advisement, in interactive learning, 85, 89
advisory board, 14–15, 40, 130–31, 141
affiliation, need for, 25, 67, 68–69, 73, 146
anxiety, 52, 54, 76, 82, 83, 86, 131
Americans with Disabilities Act, 108
Assistive Technology Act, 108
ATA. *See* Assistive Technology Act
attention: as component of ARCS model, 27, 29, 127; categories of, 50; in case study, 128; relationship to E-V theory, 27; strategies for creating, 49–59

ARCS model, viii, 21, 23–35, 37–39, 41, 43–45, 50–51, 54, 59, 63, 72–73, 75, 81, 83, 91, 95, 98, 102–4, 108, 115, 116; case study of, 121–156. *See also* Keller, John
attribution theory, 77–79, 86, 87, 91
audience motivational analysis, 28–29, 66, 102, 109, 127–29
authentic tasks, 65

Berlyne, Daniel, 52
boredom, 50, 52
brainstorming: ARCS process, 7, 30; as strategy, 54
Brophy, Jere, 76
budget, 13, 17, 19, 31, 89, 121, 127, 130, 138, 150, 155
Buffalo Bob Smith, 10
building on existing knowledge, 70. *See also* familiarity

CAMRA. *See* Children and Media Research Advancement Act
Cariglio, Michael, 125

| 171 |

challenge, 68, 80, 82, 85, 92, 96, 98, 134, 150
Children and Media Research Advancement Act, 112–13
Children's Online Privacy Protection Act, 109–10
Children's Television Act, 107, 110–11, 122
Children's Television Workshop, viii, ix; background/early leaders, 9. *See also* Sesame Workshop; CTW Model
children, as presenters, 65
choice(s), 5, 71, 99, 137
clarity, of objectives, 65, 80, 86, 115
competence, 5, 31, 68, 90, 96, 97, 99, 100, 134
concept map, as strategy, 55, 88
confidence: as component of ARCS model, 27, 75–93; categories of, 81; constructs related to, 75–81; in case study, 128, 134; relationship to E-V theory, 27; strategies for creating, 81–90
constructivism, 55
content: analysis, 103; as related to curriculum, 38–39, 67; chunking, 79, 84, 92; commercial, 58
control, providing sense of, 5, 26, 80, 85, 87, 88, 115. *See also* locus of control
convergence media, 107, 111–112, 113, 114, 117
Cooney, Joan Ganz, 9
COPPA. *See* Children's Online Privacy Protection Act
Creative Media Solutions, 126, 136, 138, 141
creativity, 132–38, 144, 152, 155
Csikszentmihalyi, Mihaly, 79, 86. *See also* flow (theory)
CTA. *See* Children's Television Act
CTW model, x; applying the, 9–21; used with ARCS Model, 32, 34, 37–45, 116; used in case study, 121–156. *See also* Children's Television Workshop
curiosity, 132; background on, 52; research on, 53; strategies for stimulating, 54–56, 99; zone of, 53. *See also* inquiry arousal
curriculum, 15–16

data collection methods, 16, 66, 82, 145, 152. *See also* focus groups; observation; questions; time on task
Day, Hy, 52
design (as process), 38, 40–41, 136–40
diversity, 131, 137, 147
Dopke, MariRae, 126, 127, 131

edit decision list (EDL), 43
effort: as measure of motivation, 1, 25, 33; attribution to, 24, 26, 31, 77–78, 86, 87, 91, 135; equating with success/results, 87, 137; factors affecting, 24
enthusiasm, as strategy, 56, 69, 85, 89
equity, 101, 135; strategies for promoting, 101. *See also* satisfaction
E-V theory. *See* expectancy-value theory
evaluation, 20, 43, 107, 140. *See also* formative research/evaluation; summative evaluation
expectancy (expectation) for success, 6, 26–27, 75, 81, 84, 91, 103–4, 116. *See also* confidence; expectancy-value theory
expectancy-value theory, 7, 25–26, 34, 72–73, 75, 77, 95, 104, 108, 115
exploration: as quest for knowledge, 52, 56; learning by, 55, 60; opportunities for, 54, 69, 115; related to motivation, 96, 99
extrinsic motivation, 6, 97, 129

INDEX

extrinsic rewards, 4, 6, 31, 91, 97, 98, 104; strategies for providing, 100–101. *See also* satisfaction

failure syndrome, 76
Falcon, Errol, 10
familiarity, 63, 69, 128; strategies for generating, 70–71, 73. *See also* relevance
FCC. *See* Federal Communications Commission
Federal Communications Commission, 110
Federal Trade Commission, 109
feedback: attributional, 86; informative/corrective, 69, 79, 84–85; positive, 97, 100; timing of, 87
flexibility: as measure of creativity, 133; in design, 56, 69, 89; in learning requirements, 81, 82
Flagg, Barbara, 18, 19
flow (theory), 79–81, 85, 86
focus groups, 18, 32, 38, 114, 117, 145, 146, 147, 149, 150
formative research/evaluation: case study example, 143–52; methods, 19; primary goal of, 20; role and issues, 18, 43
front-end analysis, 13, 38–39, 126–29, 130
frustration, 131, 151. *See also* anxiety
FTC. *See* Federal Trade commission

goal orientation, 63–64; strategies for creating, 65–66
goals and objectives: educational/curriculum, 15–16, 20, 21, 132–33; learning vs. performance, 81–82, 92; motivational, 24, 29, 31–33, 34, 126, 128, 129, 134–35
Grabowski, Barbara, 66, 88
guidance, 6, 54, 85. *See also* feedback

humor, use of, 51, 133, 146, 148

individual differences, 53, 54, 55, 128
inquiry arousal, 52–56. *See also* curiosity
instructional design: defined, 24; relationship to ARCS model, 23
integrative development approach, 37–45; concept map of, 39; example of, 126
interactive media/technologies, 5, 19, 21, 52, 55, 69, 80, 84, 85, 86, 99, 111, 113, 156
interactivity, 56, 88, 111, 112, 115, 129, 156
intrinsic motivation, 5, 95–96, 99, 152. *See also* motivation, satisfaction, intrinsic reinforcement
intrinsic reinforcement, strategies for stimulating, 98–100. *See also* satisfaction

Keller, John, ix, 23–25, 28, 30, 33, 34, 56, 75, 82–83, 84, 86, 95, 101, 115. *See also* ARCS model
Koszalka, Tiffany, 66

learned helplessness, 26, 79, 83, 85, 91
The Learning Channel, 125, 151
learning disabilities, 79
learning environment, 55, 68, 80, 81, 83, 85, 89, 92, 99
learning styles, 24, 30, 57, 60, 66, 69, 71, 82, 85
learning requirements, 81; strategies for addressing, 82–83. *See also* confidence
Lesser, Gerry, ix, 9, 10–12, 57, 130
LOC. *See* locus of control
locus of control, 78, 91, 97, 98. *See also* attribution theory
Loewenstein, G., 53
luck, attribution to, 26, 78, 91

Maslow, Abraham, 25
Maslow's hierarchy, 25, 67
Maw & Maw, 53
McClelland, David, 25, 27, 67, 146
McCormick, Moira, 126, 156
message design, 87–88
modeling, 56, 69, 88–89, 92, 99, 137
Morriset, Lloyd, 9
motivation: and ARCS model, 23–24, 49–61, 63–73, 75–92, 95–104, 108, 144; applied to case study, 144–145, 149, 151; applied to websites, 114–16; continuing, 27, 41, 95, 99, 103; defined, 3, 4; essential ingredients, 4; integrated with CTW model, 37–45; intrinsic vs. extrinsic, 5; measuring, 7
motivational design, viii, 23, 28–34, 37–38, 44, 99, 115, 127, 136
motivational profile, x, 29, 129. *See also* audience motivational analysis
motive matching, 63, 66–69, 73
music: as strategy, 49, 50, 51, 57, 58, 139, 144, 146, 149; production of, 42, 43, 138

needs. *See* achievement motivation theory
needs assessment, 13. *See also* front-end analysis
The New Howdy Doody Show, 10

observation, as research method, 16, 19, 31, 145, 150
online focus groups, 18, 38. *See also* focus group

pacing, in media, 85, 86, 129, 131, 145, 149
Palmer, Edward, 11, 49
Pappyland as a case study, 121–156
participation, audience, 111, 121, 126, 132, 139, 156

perceptual arousal: defined, 50; strategies for creating, 50–51. *See also* attention
performance: factors affecting, 25, 28; measuring, 40, 82
persistence, as measure, 33, 85. *See also* effort
personal responsibility, 86, 91; strategies for fostering, 86–90. *See also* confidence
pilot-test, 32
planning, 13. *See also* front-end analysis
power, need for, 25, 67, 68, 73
predictability. *See* repetition
preproduction, 42. *See also* production
problem-based learning (PBL), 55, 60, 66
production: development, 139–40; as process, 41–43; research, 17–18, 41, 138–39; value, 126
program elements, in case study, 146–47

question-asking behavior, 12, 26, 55
question(s), as strategy, 30, 54, 55, 56, 60, 146, 155

recognition, of accomplishment, 6, 96, 100, 101, 104, 129, 139, 141, 155
repetition, as strategy, 147
relevance: as component of ARCS model, 27, 63; categories of, 63; in case study, 128; relationship to E-V theory, 27; strategies for creating, 64–72
return on investment (ROI), 112
rewards. *See* extrinsic rewards
role models. *See* modeling
Roberts, Eric, 127
Rotter, Julian, 78

satisfaction: in case study, 129, 135; categories of, 98; as component of

ARCS model, 27; constructs related to, 96–98; relationship to E-V theory, 27, 102, 103; strategies for creating, 98–101

self-efficacy, 76, 83, 91, 98
self-fulfilling prophecy, 76–77, 91
self-motivation, 96. *See also* intrinsic motivation
self-regulation, 87, 92
sequencing, 15, 85, 89
Sesame Workshop, 9, 21
SFP. *See* self-fulfilling prophecy
Small, Dr. Ruth V, 23, 127, 140
S.O.S. For Information Literacy, 17
spokesperson, qualities of, 69, 83
strategies: adaptive, 69, 82; process of designing, 30–32. *See also* attention; relevance; confidence; satisfaction
success opportunities, 84; strategies for creating, 84–86. *See also* confidence
summative evaluation, 20, 143
support materials, 85, 150

task difficulty, attribution to, 26, 78, 91

time on task, 25, 33, 85, 152
TLC. *See* The Learning Channel
Torrance, E. Paul, 133
transitions, use of, 19, 58

value, creating, 6–7, 25, 27, 65–66, 69, 72, 128, 134. *See also* expectancy-value theory; relevance
variability/variety, strategies for creating, 30, 50, 51, 56–58, 59, 147. *See also* attention
Vroom, Victor, 7

Web Accessibility Initiative (WAI), 108
WebMAC for Children's TV Websites, 113–16; evaluation tool, 157
Weiner, Bernard, 77. *See also* attribution theory
World Wide Web Consortium (W3C), 108
Writer's Notebook, 16, 21, 41, 135–36

Young, James Webb, ix

ABOUT THE AUTHOR

Marilyn P. Arnone is director of educational media at the Center for Digital Literacy, Syracuse University. Dr. Arnone also consults and produces children's media through her company, Creative Media Solutions, in Oriental, North Carolina. She has worked in various roles, including creator, producer, instructional designer, and director of evaluation on numerous video, multimedia, and broadcast projects. Her research interests center on exploring children's curiosity and learning in interactive media environments. She has published in leading journals in her field, has authored or coauthored seven books, presents at conferences nationwide, and teaches courses and seminars as an adjunct professor at Syracuse University School of Information Studies. Dr. Arnone received her B.S. degree from Emerson College with a communications concentration, her master's degree in education from Harvard Graduate School of Education focusing on research in children's television and human development, and her doctorate from Syracuse University School of Education in instructional design, development, and evaluation.